A HISTORY OF THE ECLECTIC SOCIETY OF PHI NU THETA, 1837–1970

A HISTORY OF THE

Eclectic Society

OF PHI NU THETA,

1837–1970

WILLIAM B. B. MOODY (1959)

WESLEYAN UNIVERSITY PRESS Middletown, Connecticut

Published by Wesleyan University Press,

Middletown, CT 06459

© 2007 by William B. B. Moody

CIP data is available from the Library of Congress.

ISBN-13: 978-0-8195-6840-3

ISBN: 0-8195-6840-6

Printed in the United States of America

5 4 3 2 1

CONTENTS

Photo galleries follow pages 48 and 146. Unless otherwise noted, all illustrations are courtesy of the Archives at Olin Library, Wesleyan University.

TO THE READER

As undergraduates at Wesleyan University in the late 1950s, many of us felt our primary loyalty to the fraternity to which we belonged. It was the center of our life outside the classroom. We ate there, socialized there, and became a part of a tradition that meant a lot to many, if not most of us who joined fraternities. That was particularly the case for those of us who joined the local Wesleyan fraternity known formally as the Eclectic Society of Phi Nu Theta. It had a history dating back to the early days of the university and was always among the strongest houses on campus. It had a serious intellectual core, although the social aspects of fraternity life were not slighted. Every president of the university who had graduated from Wesleyan up to that time had been an Eclectic. Names famous in Wesleyan history were most often those revered in Eclectic as heroes of the House. When I graduated from Wesleyan in 1959, I remember pledging to myself that I would make my first financial contribution to the House and my second to the university.

Within ten years, the fraternity we knew as Eclectic had radically changed. Gone were traditions that had informed more than 130 years of undergraduate fraternity life. A crisis had occurred—not only in Eclectic but in a number of other houses as well. Some survived more or less intact; others, like Eclectic, continued in greatly altered form; and some disappeared completely.

This present effort is an attempt to trace the history of Eclectic from its founding to the years when it changed so radically in the late 1960s, to examine themes and patterns in the life of the Fraternity and to posit some theories as to why it ceased to exist in its old form. In the words of the old hymn, "Time like an ever flowing stream bears all her sons away," as is inevitably happening to those who remember the old Eclectic. There should be some record for those who may wonder why there is such a grand porticoed structure at 200 High Street in Middletown and what the strange names on the badge chiseled into the lintel over the door signify.

In writing this, I am greatly indebted to the late Paul North Rice (1910),[1] who was one of the grand old men of Eclectic during my undergraduate days. He continued the work of Eric McCoy North (1909), who began a history of the Fraternity for its hundredth anniversary in 1937. Brother North was obliged to give up the project because of professional obligations in Europe. Paul North Rice assumed the responsibility and covered the years through the 1860s in great detail. He relied on another grand old man of Eclectic, Professor Morris B. Crawford (1874), for the history of the 1870s. I have incorporated these manuscript works with minor changes into this present effort. Any errors are, of course, entirely my fault. From the 1880s on (and for some verification of earlier information), I am relying on the Eclectic archival collection of the Olin Library and the wonderfully cooperative spirit of the staff there, particularly Suzy Taraba '77, University Archivist and Head of Special Collections, and her staff, particularly Patricia Stark and Valerie Gillispie. A group of stalwart alumni rescued the Society's records from the Fraternity House and turned them over to the university archives when it appeared that little if any care was being devoted to preserving them. I am deeply indebted to those Socratic Literary Society members, too. For help with Greek titles and definitions, I am most grateful for the help of the Rev. Cynthia Walter of Christ Church Parish, Kensington, M.D., and Professor Kate K. Gilhuly '86 of the Wellesley College Classics Department.

Finally, I would like to thank all the brother Eclectics who responded to my pleas for input to this history and particularly Somerville ("Spud") Parker (1956) and David Potts (1960), University Historian, who reviewed the prose and offered suggestions for changes or additions. I owe a huge debt of gratitude to my wife, Janet Cline-Moody, who contributed her editorial skills to the effort and put up with my long stretches at the computer and occasional absences in Middletown. Without their help and encouragement, this volume would never have been completed.

William B. B. Moody (1959)
Bethesda, Maryland

GLOSSARY

Agogus	An officiant at initiations (Gr. "One who accompanies")
Alpha Chapter	The chapter at Wesleyan
Alpha Club	The dining club of the Fraternity
Appointments	Schedule of members assigned to participate in literary exercises at regular meetings
AR	Alumni Record, published every ten years through 1980
Beta Chapter	The chapter at Ohio Wesleyan (1848–60)
B.L.G.	Bare Legged Goddess, an informal organization of juniors and seniors dedicated to harassing sophomores, abolished in 1914.
B.O.D.	Board of Directors of the Socratic Literary Society consisting of resident Socrats charged with handling day-to-day matters and headed by a Chairman
Charter Gag	A preinitiation event that was as close to hazing as anything at Eclectic was in the 1950s (see chapter 13)
Choragus	Song leader (Gr. "Choral leader")
Delegation	Members of the same class within the Fraternity
Dicastes	An officiant at initiations (Gr. "Judge or juror")
Eclectic	Name of the Fraternity in common parlance, also "Phi Nu Theta"
Eclectic Hall	Formal name of the meeting room
Eclectic Repository	Collected and bound volumes of writings that formed part of literary exercises
Eclectic Society of Phi Nu Theta	Formal name of the Fraternity
Elephant Room	Common name of the waiters' dining room
Epistoleus	Corresponding secretary and equivalent of the president of the Society, elected in earlier days for a term and in later days for a year (Gr. "Secretary")

Gamma Chapter	The chapter at Dickinson (May–July 1852)
Goat Room	Eclectic Hall at 200 High Street in common parlance from at least 1911
Gr.	Greek (i.e., from the classical Greek)
Grammateus	Secretary responsible for taking minutes at meetings and acting as parliamentarian (Gr. "Secretary or registrar")
Guttering	The forceful expulsion of a member from the dining hall for some egregious violation of decorum (e.g., getting pinned). Carried out by freshmen who would deposit the offender in the gutter outside the House or naked in the fireplace (earlier days) or in a cold shower on the second floor (latter days—until 1960)
Kerux	An officiant at initiations (Gr. "Herald, crier, or messenger")
Myontes	An officiant at initiations (Gr. "Mystic or contemplator")
n	Nongraduate, e.g., "A. B. Smith (1879n)"—in the class of 1879, but did not graduate with the class
Phi Nu Theta	Name of the Fraternity in common parlance, also "Eclectic"
Proedros	Presiding officer at regular meetings and in the dining hall, rotated among seniors on a weekly basis (Gr. "President or one who sits in the first place")
Quadrennial	Public literary exercises conducted by four fraternities in rotation at graduation time (mid–nineteenth century)
Quinquecennial	Successor to the Quadrennial literary exercises and so named because the rotation was among five fraternities; abolished in 1892
SATC	Student Army Training Corps, an organization including nearly all able-bodied undergraduates, formed in October 1918 to further the World War I effort

SLS	Socratic Literary Society, the graduate arm of Eclectic, formally chartered by the State of Connecticut in 1870
Socrats	Name of the Socratic Literary Society and/or its members in common parlance
Sub rosa	Dinner or other function conducted in silence (originally referred to something kept private or secret, but modified by use at Eclectic)
Thesaurophylax	Treasurer (Gr. "Guardian of the treasury")
Thyronus	An officiant at initiations (Gr. "Doorkeeper")

CHAPTER 1

THE FOUNDING OF
THE ECLECTIC SOCIETY
OF PHI NU THETA

ctober 1837 was traditionally celebrated by Eclectics as the time of founding of the Eclectic Society of Phi Nu Theta, the first fraternity at Wesleyan University to maintain continuous existence as a four-year fraternity. Like many other historical events important to succeeding generations, the exact details of the founding are shrouded in uncertainty. Indeed, the official recognition of its existence by the faculty and its adoption of the name "Eclectic"[1] probably did not take place until 1838, although the society seems certainly to have been in existence as a less formal organization during the previous year.

It is unfortunate that the formal records of the Society do not run back quite to its actual founding and that the early history was not carefully written up while its founders were still alive. There are, however, a half dozen sources that can serve as a basis for informed conjecture. Professor Morris B. Crawford (1874) probably knew more about the fraternity than another person living when Eric North (1909) and Paul North Rice (1910) compiled their manuscript history of the early years in preparation for the 1937 Centennial. Professor William North Rice (1865) edited the first directory and expressed at various times his convictions as to the founding of the fraternity. Judge George G. Reynolds (1841), at the request of Professor Crawford, put in writing in June 1903 certain recollections of his about the early history of Eclectic. A month earlier, in May 1903, the Reverend Willard M. Rice (1837), one of the founders, had made certain statements for the record concerning the origins of the Society, which were written down in the presence of Cyrus D. Foss (1854), president of the university 1875–80. A letter from H. M. Johnson (1839) dated December 24, 1840, also bears on the question, as do letters from Jonathan Coe (1839) and Charles Collins (1837).

The dictated statement of Dr. Willard Rice is of significance, as it came from one of the founders. In part he said:

The Eclectic Society had its origin in an informal meeting of four members of the Class of 1837—Aaron H. Hurd, Charles Collins, Daniel Curry and Willard M. Rice. . . . Each of the persons mentioned above matriculated at Wesleyan in 1835. . . . During the fall and winter of 1835–36, we were in the habit of meeting together in each other's rooms—first, for the purpose of assisting each other in matters connected with our regular college studies and, secondly, for other literary work. There were also social features connected with these meetings, which ordinarily were held on Saturday evenings.

There were other students in the classes of 1835, 1836, 1837, and 1838 who were accustomed to meet occasionally with us. . . . The meetings which I have mentioned continued to be held during my senior year.

In March, 1837, Mr. Collins and myself were examined by the Faculty and by a "Committee for Graduation"—the Class graduating in August, 1837—in order that Mr. Collins, who had been elected Principal of the Augusta High School, Augusta, Maine, and myself, who had been elected Teacher of Latin and Greek in the same institution, might at once enter upon the duties of these respective positions.

We left Middletown about the end of March 1837 and took up the work in Augusta. In August we returned to Middletown for the commencement exercises. . . . During our attendance upon these commencement exercises, Messrs. Collins, Curry and myself were frequently together. One of our number, Curry, I think, suggested that it might be a bond of union in the future between us, the undergraduates and the Institution, if our informal Association took on a more formal character. For the purpose of carrying out this suggestion, conferences were held with the undergraduates who had been in the habit of meeting with us. The result was that a formal organization was effected in October, 1837, I think, although it may have been a little later. I feel quite sure, however, that it was in October . . .

Soon after [commencement], I received a letter from Dr. Fisk, President of Wesleyan, informing me that I had been elected

Tutor in that institution. I accepted the appointment and returned to Middletown in November. I found that, as already stated, the formal organization of the Association had taken place.

In those days there were two recognized literary societies—the Philorhetorian and the Peithologian. There had also been private associations, but these had been rather frowned upon by the Faculty, as they had tended, the Faculty thought, not altogether for the moral good of the Institution or the students. The members would meet in their rooms and would then, perhaps, go downtown and have a pretty high time; therefore, the Faculty discouraged all such secret societies.

There was no formal recognition of Eclectic by the Faculty until late in the year 1837; then it was authorized. Very soon thereafter the Mystics were formed, perhaps the same year—"The Mystic Seven" they styled themselves. The Mystics are reputed to have been founded in 1837, but some of the most careful historians [say] they cannot trace it back farther than 1838.

The Greek letter name was adopted when the Society was formally recognized by the Faculty. Both the Greek letter name and the name "Eclectic" were used in 1840, before I left Middletown.

The above would seem conclusive proof of the date of the organization of the Fraternity, were it not that Dr. Rice made his statement almost seventy years after the events he was discussing, while in the following letter, written December 24, 1840, from St. Charles College in Missouri, Hermann M. Johnson (1839) definitely states that it was in the fall of 1838 that the plan of the Eclectic Fraternity was approved by the faculty:

Greetings to the Fraternity—kind, thankful greetings. Your welcome letter came like the kind voice of brothers at home, to one who is far away. To hear of your prosperity was good, and that your lookings-forth are cheery, even better.

There seems to have been much opposition raised to our unpretending little band. This I am sorry to hear: not that I fear you will be subdued or that you will not maintain a respectable, if not the first, stand among rival claimants for the honor of being— in the true sense of the word—"Eclectic," but because, to have so many clubs in an institution, is not advantageous, and secondly, the original object of our association is, in some measure, defeated.

The object, not only of those who first of the students, consulted in regard to the matter, but, of the faculty, was to establish a new organization from materials so selected, and with the avenues so guarded, that it should not only be so deemed, but in fact, *be*, a privilege to gain admission—in short to create a literary distinction by founding a society, to bear the badge of which, should be a *literary honor*. When we first laid before Professor Smith our half-formed plan, we had not aimed so high, or at least had not had the boldness to express, even to one another, our forthgoing thoughts as reaching so far. Professor S. very kindly [received] our proposal; helped somewhat to give direction to our maturing purposes; and encouraged us to set our standards high. He said he long wished a distinctive and acknowledged society of the character then contemplated. Indeed, the Faculty had, once at least, I think more times, discussed the propriety and settled that question, and had agreed on the desirability and had come nearly to the acting resolution of causing to be established just such a society; and now that the students had started, he was glad to aid them. He conferred with Dr. Fisk—this was during the fall term of 1838,—our plan met his approval; it was presented to the Faculty in board, and was agreed to them by them.

There was then a question, whether to establish an original and independent society, or to seek a union with some one of standing fame. But little preference was felt by any; but as Dr. Fisk and Professor Smith and I, too, were already members of Phi Beta Kappa, it was decided to apply for a branch of that. The result of that application I have never heard, but suppose it unsuccessful.

Now you see that among the contentions of so many and petty clubs, the high objective contemplated is, if not overlooked, at least rendered almost impracticable; and hence the second cause of my regret. Our chief cause was to render *our own loved Wesleyan*, as much as possible the center of literary attractions and operations for our community, and to encourage emulation by setting up a high mark to aim at.

In his manuscript history of Eclectic's early days, Paul North Rice speculated on the mismatch between these two accounts: Dr. Rice can hardly have been mistaken in his recollections of the informal meetings of students that took place from 1835 to the summer of 1837. In view of the conference held by himself, Collins and Curry with undergraduates at commencement time in 1837 as to forming an organization for the perpetuation of the meetings that had been held under their leadership prior to their graduation, it is hardly conceivable that, when he returned to Middletown as tutor in November 1837, he should not have informed himself as to whether such an organization had been started. It is quite possible, however, that his memory failed him when he stated that formal recognition of Eclectic by the faculty took place late in the fall of 1837. The Johnson letter, being written so near the date, would seem to be rather conclusive evidence that formal recognition by the faculty did not take place until 1838.

The minutes of the Wesleyan faculty from July 9, 1836, until well into the 1840s were examined by Paul North Rice, but no formal faculty recognition of the Eclectic Fraternity, nor of the Mystical Seven, nor of any similar organization appeared. To be sure, the minutes are very short, often giving little beyond faculty attendance and such statements as "Reported the Delinquencies." On October 25, 1837, about the time that the faculty might well have commented on the organization of a fraternity that was to play so large a part in the development of Wesleyan, their minds seem to have been entirely occupied with the matter of discipline. An unusually long minute of that date states in part:

> The case of Benjm. W. Britt, one of the students, was considered, who on the night of Friday last twentieth inst. shaved off the mane and tail of the President's horse and then tied him up in the Chapel, affixing to his (i.e., the horse's) back a wicked & blasphemous notice, and being convicted of said acts, he was expelled.

There was considerable discussion among older alumni as late as the 1950s as to whether Eclectic or the senior honor society know as "The Mystical Seven" was founded first. Paul North Rice addresses this point in his manuscript, but without going into the details, it appears clear that both organizations were founded at about the same time, although Eclectic retained its name, purpose, and basic structure until at least 1968, while Mystical Seven went through a number of permutations before finally settling on its original name, but as a senior honor society, in 1881.

If there is some doubt as to the actual date when the Eclectic Society was founded, there is less doubt as to who the actual founders were. According to the statement of Dr. Willard Rice, the suggestion of a formal organization came from the members of the class of 1837 shortly after their graduation. The real initiators, then, appear to be Charles Collins, Daniel Curry, and Willard Martin Rice. While the suggestion for a society came from them, the actual founders of an undergraduate society could only be undergraduates. It is interesting to note that each of these three initiators was later elected to honorary membership in the fraternity: Rice in 1847, Collins in 1852, and Curry not until 1865. This, of course, indicates that they were not considered to be members prior to their election as honorary members.

David Patten (1834) and Moses Scudder (1837) were initiated as graduates. The same is true of the two Eclectics of the class of 1838, J. L. Alverson and Edward Cooke, who did not join until 1857 and 1854, respectively. Paul North Rice observes that the fact that no members of the class of 1838 were initiated as undergraduates is another reason to believe that no formal organization of Eclectic took place before the fall of 1838. It is highly unlikely that the Society, formed at the suggestion of three members of the class of 1837 shortly after their graduation, would have included no member of the senior class.

Brother Rice concludes that the actual founders of the formal organization were members of the classes of 1839 and 1840. No minutes of the Eclectic prior to 1846 have been discovered. The main source of extant information on early membership is the *Catalogue of the Eclectic Fraternity* published in 1865 by William North Rice (1865), Stephen Henry Olin (1866), and Henry D. Harrower (1867). A copy of the *Catalogue* preserved initially in the safe in the fraternity house and then transferred to the archives of the university bears an inscription by William North Rice:

We found no records of the Society earlier than the year 1838–39, and we give credit in the numbers in the body of the work and in the Greek letters in the index to no one as entering the Society earlier than that year. The older members are very positive that the Society did start in 1837. I suspect that there was a period in which the Society was rather loosely organized and that, later, a more definite organization was effected.

The inscription then goes on to explain the coding of the numbers mentioned above (indicative of the course year in which the member joined the fraternity and any academic distinction he achieved) and the significance of the Greek letters (the year of the Society in which the member joined—1836–37 counting as the first year). Marked with the Greek letter "gamma" are seven members of the class of 1839 and three of the class of 1840:

Lester Mumford Clark (1839)
Jonathan Coe (1839)*
Clark Titus Hinman (1839)*
Hermann Merrills Johnson (1839)*
Ichabod Marcy (1839)
Joshua Newhall (1839)*
Humphrey Pickard (1839)
Loranus Crowell (1840)
John Harrison Goodale (1840)
Chester Dorman Hubbard (1840)*

Paul North Rice concludes that these ten men may fairly be considered the founders of Eclectic, and his logic is hard to fault. All, he notes, were leaders while in college and afterward. Seven were elected to Phi Beta Kappa, and all enjoyed long and successful careers, particularly in church and education. A list purporting to be of members joining prior to June 11, 1847, states that five of the members listed above (starred) joined the Fraternity on September 13, 1838. If the list is genuine, and Brother Rice opines that it is, this is the earliest reference to a formal induction of members—and could be construed as the formal date of the founding of the Fraternity. It accords with other statements of first members with references to an informal period of meetings as early as 1836 and a more formal organization in the fall of 1838.

The flag of the Fraternity, which used to fly on festive occasions, bore the distinctive scroll/key emblem of the Society and the date "1837." It seems a reasonable compromise between 1835 (the first references to the meetings which led to the founding) and the date of September 13, 1838, discussed above. At one time there was acrimonious debate about the exact year and date, especially between Eclectics and members of the Mystical Seven Fraternity. Now that so very much has changed and the continued existence of fraternities in any form at Wesleyan is in question, it would seem mere quibbling to argue further. Vivat 1837!

CHAPTER 2

THE 1840S THE FIRST DECADE

uch of the discussion of the founding of Eclectic in the previous chapter revolved around individuals who joined the Society and influenced its development. The same is true concerning the history of the following decade. Many Eclectics of these early years became legendary figures for succeeding generations. One of these was Judge George Greenwood Reynolds (1821–1913) of the class of 1841. Almost to this day, students who frequented the Eclectic House at 200 High Street knew his face. His portrait occupied the place of honor over the fireplace in the library, for it was he who was the largest single donor of funds which made possible the building of the House in 1907.[1] Paul North Rice (1910), the author of the manuscript on which so much of this account of the early years of the Fraternity depends, knew him personally and recounts remarks the judge made on the occasion of the celebration of his ninetieth birthday in 1911:

> I was one of the first members after the Society started, but not the first initiate. The class of 1841 were the first initiates. Three of us entered sophomore year: [George] Landon, [George W.] Allen, and myself. Landon and Allen went in [i.e., joined] the first term, but I hung along until just before the end of the year. Then C. D. Hubbard and Loranus Crowell told me [of my election]. My exultation can be imagined.

Judge Reynolds also incarnates another trend that characterized Eclectic well into the twentieth century: the recurrence of names from generation to generation. His son Frank Reynolds (1868), grandson George Greenwood Reynolds II (1905), and great-grandson Blake Greenwood Reynolds (1936) all joined the fraternity in their undergraduate years.

The judge's comments on his initiation were cited by Paul North Rice as follows:

On the night when I was to be admitted to the distinguished privilege of such a literary and scholarly association, I was introduced into a room in North College, Middle Section, third story front—I think it was the rooms occupied by Marcy and Crowell. Being born out of time, I was the only newcomer. Receiving a cordial handshake and a welcome from the brethren, I took a modest seat and witnessed literary exercises, I presume very much like those in operation now. They were at that time in the habit of having essays, criticisms, and written—and I think sometimes oral—debates.

The room I have mentioned was our regular meeting place. We were tenants at sufferance, without furniture and without stationery. We had a President and a Secretary—and perhaps a Treasurer, but his position must have been a sinecure, and at all events, they all flourished under English names. The world never saw a finer example of "plain living and high thinking."

Two things particularly to note in Judge Reynolds's recollection are the venue for the meeting and its format. In these early days of the Society, meetings were held in student rooms. It was not until much later that Eclectic, like the other fraternities, acquired a clubhouse—and then only after a period of renting a room or rooms on Main Street. The literary exercises conducted at meetings were from the beginning a part of Eclectic tradition and their format, while varying in detail over the years, retained their basic outline unchanged until the 1960s.

Commencement in 1839 meant the graduation of seven of the thirteen members (G. W. Allen having already left college). During the year 1839-40, the remaining members initiated two seniors, four juniors, and two sophomores. One of the seniors was Joseph Cummings (1840), the first Wesleyan graduate to serve as president of the university. In fact, as of this writing, four of the five presidents of the university who have been Wesleyan graduates were Eclectics—Joseph Cummings (1840), Cyrus D. Foss (1854), John W. Beach (1845) and Edwin D. Etherington (1948). Doug Bennet '59 somehow managed to be elected president without being an Eclectic (he was an Alpha Chi Rho/EQV).

The academic achievements of the early Eclectics were truly outstanding. With few exceptions, the number one (valedictorian) and number two (salutatorian) positions in the graduating classes in the 1840s were Eclectics, and Eclectics contributed many of the members elected to Phi Beta Kappa. In fact, there was discussion for a while of the Fraternity's applying to Phi Beta Kappa for affiliation. An application was actually drafted in 1843 or 1844, but nothing came of it and the discussion was definitely dropped when the Connecticut Gamma Chapter of Phi Beta Kappa was founded at Wesleyan in July 1845 as an honorary fraternity. Many Eclectics held dual membership from the very beginning of Phi Beta Kappa at Wesleyan. The only serious regular fraternity rival in the realm of scholarship for many years was the Xi Chapter of Psi Upsilon, founded originally as Kappa Delta Phi in 1840, then changing its name to Kappa Sigma Theta in 1841, and finally being accepted as the Wesleyan chapter of Psi Upsilon in 1843. Paul North Rice sums up the relationship between to first two regular fraternities at Wesleyan as follows: "During the first fifty years of its existence, Psi Upsilon was the only formidable scholastic rival of Eclectic. Considering the closeness of the competition, the two fraternities were friendly indeed."

The focus of this effort is the history of Eclectic, but the Society was very closely identified with the university and could not avoid being involved in the milieu and history of the larger institution. For extensive treatment of Wesleyan's early history, David B. Potts's *Wesleyan University 1831–1910*, published in 1992, is an invaluable tool (Dave is an Eclectic, class of 1960), but Carl F. Price's earlier *Wesleyan's First Century*, published for the Centennial in 1931, should not be overlooked, especially its chapter on the fraternities. Methodism was a pervasive influence in both University and Fraternity in the early days. Many Eclectics went on to careers in the Methodist Episcopal Church. The turmoil of 1842 surrounding a student call for the resignation of President Nathan Bangs involved a number of Eclectics. One of these was John Wesley Beach (1845), who refused (at least initially) to sign an apology composed by the faculty. Those who refused to sign were to be suspended until the commencement of the next term—and then, if they had not signed with a confession of "contumacy," would be dismissed in disgrace. Beach was not dismissed. The resignation of Bangs in August 1842 evidently made the earlier faculty decision moot. Stephen Olin was elected president again (he had been unable to assume his duties because of ill health) and this time assumed those duties for a term that lasted nine years. Beach himself became Wesleyan's seventh president in 1880.

Initiates in the 1840s included such recurring names in Eclectic history as Beach (John Wesley and his brother Samuel F.), Haven (Gilbert), Ingraham (William M.), Newhall, (Fales H.), and Hyde (Ammi B.), all of the class of 1846. These early Eclectics had distinguished careers in church and academia, but they did not lack humor. I well remember one of Paul North Rice's talks to an initiation banquet in the mid-1950s. He recounted a story concerning the aforementioned Professor Ammi B. Hyde (1824–1921), long a professor of Greek at Allegheny College and later at the University of Denver. During World War I, when Professor Hyde was long since retired, some acquaintance complained to the ninety-year-old expert in Greek that the people of that country seemed to be taking a "pusillanimous and cowardly part" on the side of the Allies. He replied, "Alas, yes, the Greeks don't fight like Hell-as of old."

A number of initiatives in the 1840s reverberated through the subsequent history of the fraternity. The motto represented by the Greek letters "Phi Nu Theta" was adopted sometime between 1840 and early 1844. The badge of the fraternity, a gold watch key in the form of a scroll with both the Greek letters and the word "$Εκλεκτος$," was adopted afterward, but still before the summer of 1844, when a letter from Gilbert Haven (1846), corresponding secretary, indicates that the difficulty of engraving on a curved gold scroll had been overcome. The badge of membership had previously been a yellow ribbon worn on the lapel.

From June 11, 1846, the minutes of fraternity meetings were preserved. Those of May 1, 1847, describe another initiative which was continued in succeeding generations of Eclectics—that of "cultivation." The corresponding secretary, Daniel Steele (1848), "was instructed to write to several teachers of academies belonging to our society and ask of them information as to the students to be sent by them to our college next Commencement." Pre-frosh cultivation had early roots.

In 1848 two resignations shook Eclectic. Both members, Nathaniel J. Burton and William S. Studley of the class of 1850, joined the Mystical Seven, then functioning as a regular fraternity. Burton was asked to give his reasons for leaving. His response was that he found the "largeness" of the organization detracted from its efficiency as a literary and social institution. Eclectics of a later era may smile at the assertion. There were eighteen members before the resignations.

The decade ended on a positive note. George F. Mellen (1849), who replaced the departed William S. Studley as corresponding secretary, could write in the minutes of the annual meeting at commencement on July 30, 1849, "We can speak of no trials endured during the past year, for we have had none. We can recount no great victories achieved, for no rival has been seen. . . . The conclave that is nearest the Eclectic is the Phi Beta [Kappa], yet this must ever fall below us while marks distinguish men."

ust before commencement in 1849, a junior was initiated into the Eclectic Society of Phi Nu Theta who was to have great influence in the Fraternity and, still more, in the College. John Monroe Van Vleck (1850) was an undergraduate member for only one year, but during his long tenure as a professor at Wesleyan and loyal alumnus of the Fraternity, he was to leave an indelible imprint. "Uncle Johnny" was still invoked a hundred years later as the ideal Eclectic. Born in 1833, he became adjunct professor of mathematics in 1853. Five years later he was appointed professor of mathematics and astronomy, a post he held for forty-six years until his retirement in 1904, when he was made professor emeritus. He served three times as acting president of the university (1872–73, 1887–89, and 1896–97) and was a strong voice for curriculum reform and coeducation along with another stalwart Eclectic faculty member, William North Rice (1865). Professor Van Vleck is particularly remembered for hiring during his second interim presidency one of Wesleyan's best-known late-nineteenth-century faculty members, Woodrow Wilson. Four years after Van Vleck's death in 1912, the observatory bearing his name and dedicated to his memory was erected on Foss Hill. Professor Caleb T. Winchester '69, another giant of the era (even though a Psi Upsilon), summed up his recently deceased colleague's contributions to the University as follows: "No other man had as much to do in making Wesleyan University what it is today."

In the same year that John Monroe Van Vleck joined Eclectic, a committee of three consisting of W. F. Loomis (1851), Albert S. Hunt (1851), and A. C. Foss (1852) proposed revisions to the format of literary exercises so as to render them "more profitable and interesting, if possible." Eclectics of succeeding generations will recognize the general shape, if not the details of what the committee developed:

1. There shall be two essays before the Society at each meeting except the monthly, and the sentiment as well as the style shall be subject to criticism.

2. Two criticisms shall be read before the Society each week on the essays of the week preceding, and these shall be subject to verbal criticism.

3. Each member who has no appointment as essayist or critic shall present to the Society at each meeting some short written article, it being expressly understood that essayists and critics also may, if they choose, present these articles.

4. At the monthly meetings a review and a written discussion shall be substituted for the essays and critiques, the first of which shall not be subject to criticism. At this meeting the articles presented by each member shall be original poetry.

"Articles" did not long survive as a part of literary exercises, although their echo, "Special Topics," did.

In his manuscript chapter on the 1850s, from which much of the material in this chapter is taken, Paul North Rice commented that his chapter might have been called "The Foss Decade." Family names appear repeatedly in the annals of the Society. The committee member Archibald Campbell Foss (1852) mentioned above was followed into the Fraternity by his brother, the future president of Wesleyan, Cyrus David Foss (1854), and two years later by a third brother, William Jay Foss (1856). All three were valedictorians of their classes and leaders in fraternity and university activities. All subsequently served on the faculty for shorter or longer periods.

Ralph Chandler Harrison (1853) was initiated as a freshman and was a notable addition to the ranks of Phi Nu Theta. Less than two months after joining, he was elected secretary; he later held the offices of treasurer (twice), recording secretary, and president. He served as chairman of a committee to revise the bylaws of the Society. His report, with its notations of the most important events in the history of the Society up to that time, was gathered from minutes and documents that have since disappeared. His efforts have provided invaluable information to subsequent researchers into the early history of Eclectic. In life after graduation he followed a career in law, a calling somewhat unusual in the days of minister and educator graduates. Even more unusual, he left the East and moved to California, where he served as a member of the Board of Freeholders that framed a charter for San Francisco in 1880, chaired the Board in 1886, served as Justice of the Supreme Court of California 1891–1903, and later (1905–6) presided over a District Court of Appeals in California. Ralph C. Harrison died in 1918, but obviously made a great impression on Eclectics of the early twentieth century, most notably on Paul North Rice.

The year 1850 also witnessed an event that was much discussed among Eclectics of subsequent generations: the formal recognition of a Beta Chapter of Eclectic at Ohio Wesleyan. This 1955 initiate into the Fraternity must admit that the occasional references to a Beta chapter, the existence of fraternity badge keys bearing a "Beta" in the upper-right-hand corner, and the suggestion that other chapters may have existed or been considered were fascinating. In researching this era of Eclectic's history, this member of the Alpha Chapter discovered that another chapter, the Gamma Chapter, was indeed founded at Dickinson College in Pennsylvania in 1852 and existed for two months. The history of the ill-fated Beta (1848–60) and Gamma (1852) Chapters—along with efforts to establish other chapters—will be deferred to chapter 4, "The Crisis of the 1860s."

The first recorded effort to establish a regular meeting room appears in Ralph C. Harrison's compendium of early acts of the Society and is dated April 4, 1845. This room was in the "Mansion House" and served as a meeting space from July 2, 1845, until July 25, 1848. There was then a move to a room rented from "Ferre." In 1851 the first reference appears in Society records of efforts to procure meeting rooms on a long-term basis and dedicated to fraternity purposes with an expenditure of money involved. A committee was appointed, and in its report of September 18, 1851, it stated that a "fine room" could be rented for fifty dollars a year. By October 1851 members were fitting out the room with partitions so that the Eclectic Hall would consist of two rooms: a "sessions room" (16 by 24 feet) and an anteroom (16 by 10 feet). Beneficial occupancy occurred on February 28, 1852. The rented hall was above Ward's Shoe Store on Main Street. Mr. Ward was unwilling to grant a lease, but he did agree to give notice at an agreed-upon period before requiring the Society to vacate the premises. He also agreed to install piping for gas lighting, provided that the Society assume 10 percent of the cost of the piping. Twenty-one months later the installation of gas illumination was approved (minutes of November 19, 1853).

"Cultivation" was the term used in the mid–nineteenth century for what fraternity members a century later called "rushing." The year 1851 was a bad year for Eclectic's cultivation. Each of the three upper classes had four members. Membership was offered to three freshmen in September, and all refused. Two joined the Mystical Seven, and one, Chi Psi. Eclectic went through the year with only twelve members—all upperclassmen. The incident points up another aspect of life at Wesleyan in this era—the number of rival fraternities was growing.

On July 23, 1853, Ralph C. Chandler, president of the Society, gave a report as a member of the Committee on the Revision of the Bylaws. As a result, the following resolutions were adopted:

> That the revised Constitution and By-laws be transcribed and the name and residence at the time of joining as near as can be ascertained, together with the time of joining of each member of the Society be recorded and that hereinafter it be required of each member when he joins the Society that he record his name in the book kept for that purpose, together with his residence and the time of his joining.
>
> That it be made the duty of the Cor. Sec. to transcribe upon the pages of the record book all resolutions, by-laws and enactments of the Society and all reports of special committees when not exceeding one page of letter paper, and that, when greater than that, that the substance of the report be recorded.

The minutes then reflect that, apparently in gratitude for the passage of the resolutions, Brother Chandler "manifested his liberality by inviting all the members present to Mr. Ferrie's and treating them to the creams." Also in gratitude to my long since departed Brother Chandler, I would like to comment that through the 1950s, his committee's recommendations were still being observed.

Among the freshmen initiated on September 15, 1855, was Frederick Walter Pitkin (1858), the only Eclectic known to have become the governor of a state. He was recognized as an undergraduate for his oratorical abilities. His address on "Mahometanism" at his graduation on August 10, 1858, was acclaimed by the newspaper *Sentinel and Witness*, which commented: "This was one of the finest productions of the day in point of literary merit and delivery. Taking into consideration his age, we think he bids fair to become one of the foremost men of his class."

The prophecy was fulfilled. F. W. Pitkin, after graduating from the Albany Law School in 1859, opened a law office in Milwaukee. After serious illness in 1872 he went first to Europe and then to Colorado for his health and settled in Pueblo in 1874. His abilities were such that he was nominated on the Republican ticket for governor in 1879 and won, becoming the second incumbent in that office. He was reelected to a second term in 1881. During his tenure he had to deal with conflicts between rival railways, a turbulent uprising of the Ute Indians, and the labor unrest at the Leadville Mine. He made an unsuccessful bid for a U.S. Senate seat from Colorado in 1882, filled out his term as governor, and then returned to his law practice in Pueblo in 1883. He died on December 18, 1886.

More spacious accommodations for the Society occupied the attention of the Society in 1856. Having occupied the hall over Ward's Shoe Store since 1852, the members discussed the possibility of securing better quarters at a meeting on April 28, 1856. Four sophomores were appointed a committee "to take into consideration the propriety of changing and of examining the halls in town that may be procured." Their efforts were successful, for on May 31, 1856, it was voted that "the committee close the agreement with the owner of the future room." This room in a building on the east side of Main Street, just south of Washington Street, was to serve as Eclectic's meeting place until the house on College Place was built in 1882.

The move to the new facility did not go without incident. On June 21, 1856, the committee reported that Mr. Ward required six months' notice of the Society's intention to leave. Nevertheless, the minutes for the Annual Meeting of August 5, 1856, state that the society met in its new quarters: "The new Hall was the first object of conversation. The good taste and good sense of the committee were universally commended — and references were made to the primitive times when the members gathered in an upper room for their meetings." At the same Annual

Meeting in 1856, the matter of election of honorary members was discussed. Honorary membership had previously been decided in a somewhat haphazard fashion. The Annual Meeting meant to put it right with the following resolution, which was adopted:

> Whereas it is improper, since the election of honorary members is by annual meeting, that such election should be regulated by rules having respect to the meetings of undergraduate members. Therefore: Resolved that we recommend to the Society a repeal of Article 4th, Section 4th. In case the Society's action accord with the recommendation of the above-resolved, this Annual Meeting instruct the Cor. Sec. to notify Professor Van Vleck, Rev. R. H. Loomis, A. Vail, Esq., of the fact and furnish them with a copy of the constitution. The above-named individuals shall constitute a committee at the next Annual Meeting to bring forward a code of by-laws, both to regulate the election of honorary members and such other matters as they may judge proper to be acted upon by the annual sessions of the Society.

Surprisingly, the Society initiated Samuel Foster Upham (1856) on August 2, 1856, just a few weeks before his graduation. The move was a wise one. As Paul North Rice commented in his manuscript history of the early years, his name was familiar to generations of Eclectics "both because of his loyalty to the Fraternity and because that loyalty was passed on to his son, Francis Bourne Upham (1885), and his grandsons, Francis Bourne Upham Jr. (1915) and S. Foster Upham (1919)." The line did not stop there. His great-grandsons were also counted among Eclectics of the mid–twentieth century: Francis Bourne Upham III (1945) and Hayward Upham (1950). In the mid-1950s there was much discussion about how much weight "legacies" should carry in the rushing process. Historically, the status, called being a "born man" in earlier generations, counted for much. One can argue the rights and wrongs of the practice, but I think it fair to say that the Society benefited from the loyalty of its multigenerational members.

In the fall of 1856 the Society counted eight seniors, six juniors, and two sophomores. Cultivation resulted in the initiation of one sophomore and seven freshmen by the end of October. There were, then, twenty-four undergraduate Eclectics as the year 1856 drew to a close, a healthy number in the light of what was to transpire in the next decade. After college the members enjoyed careers mainly as prominent leaders in the Methodist Church or in education, but one of the freshman initiates, William Lawton Spaulding (1860), represented a growing trend of Wesleyan graduates who found their calling in the law. Brother Spaulding was the valedictorian of his class. In the words of Paul North Rice, "[his] brilliant career as a lawyer was cut short by his tragic death in battle in the Civil War." The war was to have a devastating effect on the whole fabric of American society and especially on many colleges and their fraternities.

"Eclectic Hall" was the formal name of the Fraternity's meeting room in the late 1950s, and most members thought of it with respect, if not a kind of awe. References to the term appear from time to time in early records of the Society, but more as simply a place than as something imbued with greater meaning. An indication appeared in the minutes of September 27, 1856, that a change might be occurring: "A vote was passed that no person be allowed to eat or drink, smoke or chew in this room." Such activities were most definitely frowned upon a hundred years later.

The number and manner of electing honorary members occupied the attention of the Annual Meeting of 1856. The undergraduates were asked to revisit the matter, which they did at a Regular Meeting on February 14, 1857, by deleting offending language from the bylaws. A week later, they adopted a further modification to the bylaws as follows: "It shall be the duty of the Corresponding Secretary to carry on a regular correspondence with the chapter or chapters of the Society, making such communication as he shall deem important or interesting to the said chapter or chapters." Professor Van Vleck found this formulation wanting and proposed the following wording at a later undergraduate meeting:

> It shall be the duty of the Cor. Sec. of each chapter at the close of every collegiate term to send to the Cor. Sec. of every other chapter a list of members initiated during the term and of the officers chosen for the succeeding term, together with an account of all proceedings of the chapter, which shall be of general interest to

the Fraternity; and it shall be the duty of each Cor. Sec. receiving this communication to record the names of the members thus reported as initiated in a book kept for that purpose.

Each chapter at its annual meeting may elect, by ballot, honorary members not exceeding three in number, from the graduates of the institution with which the chapter is connected; and the vote of all members present shall be necessary for an election.

The undergraduates approved both the suggested amendments with only one modification: that the number of honorary members elected could be four instead of three.

The implication of these actions is interesting. In the first place, one can draw the conclusion that the undergraduates of the day did not always see eye to eye with their elders, although the discussions appear always to have been polite. Second, and more important, the Fraternity was at the time a national. There was a Beta Chapter at Ohio Wesleyan formally recognized in 1850 and still functioning in 1857, and there had been a Gamma Chapter at Dickinson College for two months in 1852, as mentioned earlier in this chapter. The idea was evidently still very much alive that Eclectic would continue as a national fraternity— and presumably grow. Recognition of members and coordination of actions, both serious issues of governance for the whole Society, were addressed in the amendments to the bylaws, which, however, obviously could not be the last word on such issues.

It seems strange that the new provisions of the bylaws were not observed at the Annual Meeting of August 1857. Loranus Crowell (1840), one of the founders, presided. Miner Raymond and William Rice were elected honorary members. Neither was a graduate of Wesleyan, which the bylaws would appear to have required. In any case, both had close associations with the university and with Methodism. Dr. Raymond was principal of Wesleyan Academy, which became known as Wilbraham Academy in 1912. That institution provided the College with its first president, Willbur Fisk, and with many entering students over the years. William Rice was then in the New England Conference of the Methodist Church and was shortly to become librarian of the Springfield (Massachusetts) Public Library. His son, William North "Billy" Rice, entered college four years later and was destined to become one of the most influential Eclectics of all time in university and fraternity affairs. Paul North Rice (Billy's nephew) commented in his manuscript history of these years that the honorary election of William Rice "made 'Billy Rice' a born man" (a later term was "legacy"). So another Eclectic clan came into being. Although the founder, Willard M. Rice (1837), was not a relative, the interrelated names of Rice, North, Mason, and Camp would recur repeatedly in Society annals for a century after the initiation of the honorary brother, William Rice.

In September 1857 only three freshmen were initiated, but among them was the valedictorian of his class, Wilbur Fisk Osborne (1861), and the salutatorian of that same class, Roswell S. Douglass (1861). Paul North Rice described Brother Douglass as one of the most loyal Eclectics. He sent six sons to Wesleyan, and all of them were Eclectics. For one reason or another the five older sons failed to remain at the college for the full four years. The youngest, Gordon Clark Douglass (1908), graduated with his class. When he rose to take part in the Class Day exercises, he was interrupted by a cheer. His white-haired father and five brothers shouted:

Here we are and here we be
We're awfully proud of Gordon C.
Douglasses present and Douglasses past
Hurrah for Wesleyan
This is the last!

As things turned out, they were wrong in their prophecy. Eclectic received a third-generation Douglass, Roswell Hoyt Douglass (1928), son of Roswell Leon Douglass (1901n).

The first mention of the Alpha Club appeared the following year in the first issue of the *Olla Podrida* that appeared on December 10, 1858. The first issue of the publication, which later became the Wesleyan yearbook, was a four-page folio costing four cents. While the name of Eclectic does not appear—probably because the Fraternity refused to participate—the Alpha Club is listed as an eating club located at the corner of Washington and Broad Streets. Its membership included eight Eclectics (of fifteen in the Society at the time), seven Mystical Seven members (of eleven), four Psi Upsilons, three Alpha Delts, and one independent. There were four other eating clubs listed (Chique

Chauque, Chronometer, Phoenix, and Pickwick). They, like the Alpha Club, were not identified with any one fraternity. Within ten years, however, they either disappeared or became associated with a particular organization. The Alpha Club, composed chiefly of Eclectics and Mystical Sevens, became the eating club of Phi Nu Theta about 1865, according to the historical annals in the Alumni Directory.

The last college year of the decade opened with only twelve undergraduate members of Eclectic: six seniors, four juniors, and two sophomores. William L. Spaulding (1860) and Edson W. Burr (1860) as well as Wilbur F. Osborne (1861) and Roswell S. Douglass (1861) were the top-ranked scholars in their respective classes. "Cultivation" was highly successful. On August 20, 1859, ten freshmen, members of the class of 1863, were initiated. One of these was William P. Hubbard (1863) from western Virginia, son of founder Chester D. Hubbard (1840), who was also a founder of the State of West Virginia. The father was present at the initiation and spoke to the undergraduates. Paul North Rice commented that it was not usual for alumni to attend initiations in those days, especially from such a great distance, and that this may well have been the first time an Eclectic took part in such a ceremony for his son.

The decade of the 1850s was a successful one for Phi Nu Theta in spite of increasing competition from other fraternities. The names of men such as J. M. Van Vleck (1850), C. D. Foss (1854), R. C. Harrison (1853), and F. W. Pitkin (1858) are an honor to both the University and the Fraternity. Scholarship continued to be the mark of the Society. In these ten years, Eclectic had five members who led their class in scholarship—A. S. Hunt, R. C. Harrison, and the three Foss brothers. No other fraternity could match that record. The most any other could boast was two.

CHAPTER 4

THE CRISIS OF
THE 1860S

he decade of the Civil War was a decade of crisis for Wesleyan, as for other colleges. The fraternities were even more deeply affected by this war than by the two world wars that followed in the twentieth century. So many men enlisted and left college that the very existence of a few fraternities was imperiled. Indeed, the Wesleyan chapters of Chi Psi and Delta Upsilon did cease to exist for a time, not being revived until 1875 and 1919, respectively.

That Eclectic did not suffer the fate of Chi Psi was in no small degree due to the energy and enthusiasm of four undergraduates: William Pallister Hubbard (1863), Henry Cruise Murphy Ingraham (1864), William North Rice (1865), and Stephen Henry Olin (1866). Especially remarkable was the influence which Billy Rice exerted almost from his initiation in 1861. The story of this decade is dominated by the reorganization of the Fraternity under his leadership.

The 1860s opened with Phi Nu Theta in good shape. The strong senior delegation included the university valedictorian, William Lawton Spalding, and salutatorian, Edson Wyllys Burr, both of the class of 1860. A smaller junior delegation included Wilbur Fisk Osborne (1861), who was to be valedictorian, and Roswell S. Douglass, who was to be salutatorian of the same class. Brother Douglass in making his report as corresponding secretary in the summer of 1860 asserted that the past year had ranked "amongst the most prosperous years of our existence."

There is a certain smugness in his discussion of the reasons why Eclectic again refused to cooperate in the publication of the *Olla Podrida*:

> The year previous to this, a College paper was published containing notices of the different societies, and at that time we declined being noticed therein. This year an attempt was made to publish a paper of like description, and our assistance was requested for

that purpose. Thinking, however, that such a paper would benefit other societies more than our own and that we should gain but little by it, the Society withheld their sanction, and the paper was *not* published—a clear instance of cause and effect showing power in the cause!

At the Annual Meeting of 1860, where this report was read, Chester D. Hubbard (1840) was chosen as president. It was voted to have a Quadrennial celebration in 1861. The Quadrennial was a kind of public literary exercise conducted by each of the four oldest fraternities in rotation and held as part of graduation ceremonies. A principal and reserve orator as well as a principal and reserve poet were elected. The Quadrennial was held on June 18, 1861, but by some mischance, none of the principals or reserves was able to appear. The edition of *Zion's Herald* (Boston's Methodist newspaper) for June 26, 1861, commented:

> On Tuesday, another large audience assembled to hear an orator and poet address one of the secret societies, but both speakers failed, a failure which was the less regretted since an impromptu, but capital address was wrung out of the heart and lips of the Rev. C. D. Foss of Brooklyn, a young Methodist minister of the New York East Conference, who so appropriately mingles the fire of old Methodism with the culture of the new that it may do no harm to refer to it.

There was earlier mention of the initiation of William P. Hubbard (1863) in the fall of 1859. The first son of an Eclectic to become a member, he carried on the tradition of his father, Chester D. Hubbard (1840), for he was the salutatorian of his class, a leader in the Fraternity during his undergraduate days, and president during his senior year. The following quotations from the Society's minutes hint that facility in (or perhaps enthusiasm for) verse was apparently not one of Brother Hubbard's strong points during his undergraduate days, although political acumen certainly was:

> September 19, 1862. Notice was given that one week from tonight a motion will be made to appoint two members weekly to favor the Society with original poems of at least 300 words.

October 3, 1862: Poetry motion taken up and carried. M. L.
Scudder (1863) and W. P. Hubbard (1863) appointed to read
poems next week.

October 17, 1862: W. P. Hubbard's poem deferred one week. M. L.
Scudder read a poem entitled "Legend of History."

October 24, 1862: W. P. Hubbard's poem deferred one week.

October 31, 1862: W. P. Hubbard's poem deferred one week.

November 7, 1862: In accordance with a notice given at the
previous meeting, a motion was made and carried that we
erase the new by-law relative to poems.

William P. Hubbard's career in politics rivaled that of his father. After short service in the Third West Virginia Cavalry, he became Clerk of the West Virginia House of Delegates. Later he became a member of the same House of Delegates, and from 1907 to 1911 he represented West Virginia in the U.S. House of Representatives.

A frequent visitor to the Fraternity, W. P. Hubbard became one of the best-known and most loved Eclectics. His flashes of wit enlightened many an annual meeting and fraternity banquet. Frederick M. Davenport (1889) liked to tell of an annual meeting when Professor Morris B. Crawford (1874) presented what he called "rough minutes." Hardly had he finished when Brother Hubbard remarked, "I move the 'rough minutes' be filed." His financial contributions to the Society and the College were significant throughout his life. He was the principal donor for the 1863 chimes, installed in the belfry of South College in 1919.

Henry Cruise Murphy Ingraham (1864) was initiated in August 1860. His contribution to saving the Society, especially through cultivation of new members in the fall of 1863, will be recounted later, but it should be noted here that he was the third member of the Ingraham family to become an Eclectic. He was preceded by his brothers Richard Ingraham (1842) and William Murphy Ingraham (1846). Perhaps no family has contributed more to Phi Nu Theta than the Ingrahams. Richard Ingraham (1842) had a son, George, in the class of 1871. William Murphy Ingraham had two sons who were Eclectics, George Seney Ingraham (1885) and Robert Seney Ingraham (1888). Three of the sons of H. C. M. Ingraham (1864) were loyal members of Phi Nu Theta: Henry Andrews Ingraham (1900), Edward Andrews Ingraham (1902), and Olin Ingraham (1904). Two of Henry Andrew Ingraham's sons also joined the Fraternity: Henry G. Ingraham (1933) and David Ingraham (1940). David Ingraham (1940) had a son, John Winthrop Ingraham (1970), who continued the family Eclectic tradition into the fourth generation.

Most of the Ingrahams have become members of the bar. H. C. M. Ingraham was for many years a distinguished lawyer in Brooklyn. From 1897 to 1911 he served Wesleyan University as a trustee, and during the period 1903–11 he was president of the Board of Trustees.

On August 29, 1861, only three freshmen were initiated; one of them was to leave college after a few months and another during his junior year. The third, however, more than any other undergraduate, helped Phi Nu Theta to weather the crisis of the 1860s. That man was William North "Billy" Rice (1865). Much of the rest of this chapter will address his influence and leadership in reorganizing and strengthening the Fraternity.

The Class of 1865 was an unusually brilliant one, but Billy Rice led in scholarship in every term of every year. In those days grades were given with an exactness which would shock students of today, or indeed of fifty years ago. A perfect score for one term was 1,000, for one year 3,000, for an entire four years 12,000. During the twenty-four years (1860–84) when grades were given in this fashion, there were twenty-eight students who scored 10,800 or higher. Only five scored more than 11,000, and of these the first three were all members of the class of 1865. The second and third were two eminent members of Psi Upsilon—Professor George L. Westgate (later professor of political and social science at Wesleyan) and the Rev. James Mudge. With a score of 11,289, William North Rice was not only high man, but his lead over the second man, Professor Westgate, was more than 100 points—a larger gap than between any other of the twenty-eight leaders.

Despite the infusion of leadership that exerted itself later in the decade, it is evident that, in the very early 1860s, the spirit of the Fraternity was not at its best. The records show that attendance at weekly meetings was far from satisfactory, and there was much lack of punctuality and fidelity in meeting appointments for literary exercises. A particularly bad showing was made in the spring of 1861. At five meetings held during March, April, and May that year, all articles that were due to be presented were excused or postponed, and at one of these meetings so few members were present that the meeting simply adjourned without further action of any kind. The trend persisted. For example, at a meeting in June 1862, where only nine members were present, the minutes report that "seven members had reports at this meeting. One performed his duty." Evidently in an effort to improve the situation, it was voted at the next meeting that "the names of the members present at each meeting be placed on the records of that meeting." This rule was observed for several years and probably contributed to the marked improvement in regularity of attendance and fidelity to obligations that later characterized the weekly meetings.

The "depression" of 1861 was reflected in the recruitment of new members, as mentioned previously. Again, during the academic year 1862–63 the addition to the membership was very small—only four in number—one of these belonging to the class of 1863. One of the four, however, was a name that was to echo through the years in the history of the College and the Fraternity—Stephen Henry Olin (1866).

The reduction in membership also reflected the times. Many undergraduates left college to join the army. Of the Eclectics in the classes of 1863, 1864, and 1865, six left college to join the Union forces. Of these, three died in service: William Alvord Fosgate and Lucius Seneca Nichols of the class of 1864 and Merritt Hoag Sherman of the class of 1865. Three others from earlier classes also gave their lives in the Union cause: James Q. Rice (1850n), Monroe Nichols (1857), and William L. Spalding (1860).

The Civil War caused nationwide financial stress as well, resulting in many students dropping out or not applying to colleges at all. The total number of students at Wesleyan declined from 150 at the beginning of the academic year 1861–62 to 112 at the beginning of the academic year 1864–65. Figures also taken from the University Catalogue show that the dearth of students lasted beyond the end of the war in 1865. The senior class of 1866 counted only sixteen members at the beginning of the academic year, and the following year the senior class numbered seventeen.

The Delegation of 1863 was exceptionally large and talented. The looming departure of those ten brothers was of considerable concern, for it would leave only ten members remaining (five rising seniors, two rising juniors, and three rising sophomores). That estimate may be too high in view of the record of attendance at the initiation meetings the following fall.

To help meet the brewing crisis, a committee of three was appointed in April 1863 "to correspond with the alumni with reference to those who are intending to enter college next year." The committee consisted of Henry C. M. Ingraham (1864), William N. Rice (1865), and Stephen Henry Olin (1866), three great names in Eclectic history.

"Cultivation" up to this time seems to have been carried on somewhat sporadically, special members being appointed from time to time to cultivate specific individuals. A step toward a better method, however, was now made by a vote whereby an individual, H. C. M. Ingraham, was appointed "chief of cultivation for the ensuing season," with the understanding "that the Society consider itself a committee of the whole subject to him." The results were gratifying. On September 4, 1863, at the first meeting after the summer vacation, "the Society tendered a vote of thanks to [Brother] Ingraham for his labors during the cultivation season." A week later, eight new members were initiated; however, the records indicate that only five active members were present to participate in the initiation of the eight. Another two members were initiated at the next meeting, and another single member at the following one, for a total of eleven new members. At each of these two later initiations, only six members of long standing were present, showing to what degree, prior to the admission of new members, the active membership had been reduced.

The crisis—at least as concerned membership—was past. Besides the Delegation of 1867 (initiated in 1863), a strong delegation was secured later in the class of 1868. Also, added strength came in a quite unusual way. As mentioned previously, the Wesleyan chapter of Chi Psi closed its doors for a while. Four strong men, who had been members of Chi Psi, joined Eclectic following the suspension of Chi Psi's chapter: Daniel G. Harriman (1864), Allen Clark (1865), Joseph H. Mansfield (1865), and William H. H. Phillips (1865). Also, in another unusual way at the time, two valued names were added to the Fraternity's list: Thomas B. Wood (1864) and Wilbur O. Atwater (1865). Both came from other colleges and became members of Phi Nu Theta.

Thus, by the commencement of 1865, when Billy Rice alone graduated at the full term of four years, his delegation numbered five (or six, depending on one's sources). The full membership of the Society then counted twenty-four. It is not difficult to imagine, however, that but for the talent, loyalty, and strenuous endeavor of a small group who faced the crisis of 1863, Eclectic, like the Chi Psi and Delta Upsilon chapters, might have disappeared temporarily, or perhaps in the case of Eclectic, forever.

Besides making great strides in new members in 1863, the Fraternity that year inaugurated a key provision that was to mark the Society for a hundred years, the systematic preservation of the papers presented at its weekly literary meetings. Toward the end of the school year 1862–63, William P. Hubbard (1863) and William North Rice (1865) were instrumental in the passing of rules requiring all articles read before the Fraternity to be written on specially designated paper and to be taken in charge by the librarian, who had the responsibility to ensure that they were bound year by year in volumes. These procedures show the emphasis the Fraternity placed on its weekly literary program. In spite of failures of individuals from time to time as to punctuality and care in meeting literary appointments, until the late 1960s a commanding tradition was handed down from college generation to college generation of maintaining as the most essential feature of the weekly meeting— a serious literary program with opportunity for, and the vigorous practice of, critical discussion of the exercises presented.

A very valuable contribution to the history of the Fraternity was made by the men of the mid-1860s in the publication of a complete and very carefully prepared catalogue of members. In June 1864, it was voted to publish such a catalogue, and a committee of four, one member from each class—Ingraham (1864), Rice (1865), Olin (1866), and Harrower (1867)—was appointed to make all arrangements for its publication. The catalogue was published in 1865 and distributed to all living alumni. Another catalogue of members was published in association with the seventieth anniversary of Phi Nu Theta in 1907 under the direction of Frederic Stewart (1908) and Eric M. North (1909), and an alphabetical list of members 1837–1931 prepared, but never published, in conjunction with the Centennial of the University in 1931. Since 1931, there has been no comprehensive listing of Eclectics developed or published, and the most recent *Alumni Directory* (2000) does not even mention fraternity affiliations, although the University's database does include that information, if provided by individual graduates. Volume 2 of this history, available to interested readers, includes a listing by delegation and alphabetical order of all initiated Eclectics 1834–1971.

An important act of the Fraternity in the academic year 1864–65 was a revision of the Constitution. On October 28, 1864, a committee consisting of Brothers W. N. Rice (1865), W. H. H. Phillips (1865), W. O. Atwater (1865), S. H. Olin (1866), and H. D. Harrower (1867) was appointed to draft a revised Constitution. At the Annual Meeting of July 18, 1865, the record indicates "Olin presented a report of the Committee on Constitution . . . [which] was adopted by the Meeting as representative of the Alpha Chapter." The new Constitution of 1865 gives the titles and duties of officers according to the usage that prevailed for the next hundred years: Proedros (weekly rotating presiding officer), Epistoleus (corresponding secretary and de facto president of the House), Grammateus (recording secretary), Thesaurophylax (treasurer), and Choragus (song leader) as officers of the Society and Agogus, Dicastes, Thyronus, Kerux, and Myontes as officiants at initiations. With the new Constitution began the custom of having each initiate subscribe to the Constitution by signing it. It was still the custom in the 1950s.

At the same July 1865 Annual Meeting which adopted the new Constitution, a resolution was introduced as follows: "Moved, in order to be in harmony with the new Constitution, it be the sense of this meeting that the establishment of [other] chapters be desirable. Carried." It may seem odd that the Constitution of 1865 made provision for other chapters, when the attitude toward expanding into a national organization definitely became negative within a few years. At this time, however, there were two serious efforts by students at Genesee College in Lima, New York, to form a chapter of Phi Nu Theta. A petition from Genesee dated January 14, 1864, listing the names of ten students in all four classes and signed by sophomore William R. Benham, was dispatched to the Alpha Chapter. It contained wording which indicated that the faculty and administration of Genesee College was dead set against secret societies and requested that all correspondence be handled very cautiously. The name "Rev. D. A. Wheelen of Auburn" was invoked as one who could initiate the new members of what would have become the Delta Chapter, if a member or members of the Alpha Chapter could not proceed to western New York State to do the honors. There is no record of such an Eclectic, but there was a Rev. Daniel A. Whedon (1845), who resided in Utica, New York, and was probably the Eclectic with whom the earnest Genesee undergraduates were in contact. The Alpha Chapter wanted no part of such an irregular arrangement and said so. A year later, the Genesee group, this time numbering seventeen in the classes of 1865 to 1868, again petitioned to become a chapter of the Society. This time they stated, "We have the assurance that it will meet with no opposition from the faculty, and it will for a long time have no opposition, save from a rapidly declining league called 'The Mystical Seven.'" The petition goes on to say that the members already exist as a private secret society, strong, although unknown to all but themselves. It recounts the academic prowess of its members and begs reconsideration of the previous rejection. The pleas were in vain. There was not to be a Delta Chapter.

There had been a Beta Chapter, however, and it existed for over ten years with a fair degree of success. It was founded at the urging of the Rev. Hermann M. Johnson (1839), one of the founders of the Alpha Chapter, who succeeded twice in aiding in the establishment of other chapters of Phi Nu Theta. He taught first at St. Charles College in Missouri (1839–42), from where he wrote the letter quoted in chapter 1 concerning the founding of the Fraternity. He then taught at Augusta College in Kentucky for two years (1842–44). While at Augusta, his counsel was sought on the Constitution being drafted for the Society. He urged provision be made for other chapters and stated in a letter of October 5, 1844, that he expected to be called to a professorship at Ohio Wesleyan University at Delaware, Ohio. He appears to have been thinking of establishing a Beta Chapter at Augusta, but opined that the new university in Ohio offered better soil for planting another branch of the Eclectic Society. He was indeed called to teach at Ohio Wesleyan University in 1844 and spent the next six years there. He wasted no time in laying the groundwork for the Beta Chapter of the Eclectic Society of Phi Nu Theta. The Wesleyan archives now possess the "Constitution and Rules of Government of the Eclectic $\Phi N \Theta$ Association Ohio Wesleyan University" dated November 4, 1844, and signed by John W. Beach (1845), president of the Alpha Chapter and later president of Wesleyan University. This Constitution limits the number of members of the Beta

Chapter to fifteen undergraduates and refers to "chapters," clearly indicating that other chapters were contemplated. The initiation ceremony parallels exactly the ceremony used by the Alpha Chapter at the time. The first meeting of the Beta Chapter was held on January 4, 1848, in Professor Johnson's rooms under authority of the 1844 charter. The report of the corresponding secretary of the Alpha Chapter for the year ending August 7, 1850, indicates that the Alpha Chapter had officially recognized the Beta Chapter earlier in the school year and that the Beta Chapter was "flourishing" and counted fourteen members.

The minutes of the Alpha Chapter of August 1, 1856, state that R. F. Crowell (1857) and Nathaniel Fellows (1858) were appointed to wait upon Burwell F. Goode to ascertain whether he was a member of the Beta Chapter at Ohio Wesleyan and, if so, to inform him that he was recognized as a member of the Alpha Chapter and invite him to attend meetings of the Middletown Chapter. Brother Goode was apparently one of two members of the short-lived Beta Chapter who transferred his membership to—or visited—the Alpha Chapter (the other being W. F. King in the summer of 1858). This appears to represent the only documented personal (as opposed to written) relationship between the two chapters.

In a letter dated April 9, 1859, W. F. King, corresponding secretary of the Beta Chapter, gave an account of the condition of the Beta Chapter eleven years after its founding. The report is glowing. Scholarship is highly regarded; every alumni tutor has been an Eclectic; literary exercises are "creditable"; and "brotherly concord is without exception." In contrast to the Alpha Chapter, the Ohio Eclectics did not use a meeting hall but had always met in one of the tutors' rooms. Brother King concluded his letter with an inquiry as to whether the founding of other chapters was under consideration and whether it would be considered appropriate to allow the faculty to inspect the chapter's Constitution.

This last comment suggests that the Beta Chapter may have been under some pressure from the faculty. The attitude of the faculty of a number of colleges of the time was not friendly to secret societies. It is quite likely that such an attitude contributed to precipitous collapse of the Beta Chapter. Despite the optimistic words of Brother King, collapse it did in little more than a year. The last initiates were recorded on June 7, 1859, and the last recorded minutes of the Beta Chapter are dated June 21, 1860. An accounting of the last days of the Beta Chapter was penned by one of its former members, W. L. Whitlock, in a letter dated May 6, 1866, to Warren L. Hoagland (1866) of the Alpha Chapter in response to earlier inquiries. Brother Whitlock states in his 1866 letter that "the Society was not continued and has now no organization." He then gives specifics:

> About the year 1860 (I do not remember the exact time), the Beta Chapter felt that if the organization was to be made profitable and as agreeable as possible to its membership, additional chapters should be formed, and its influence extended. The chapter located in this institution corresponded with the Alpha Chapter on this subject, and the latter would not agree to an extension. Some of the members became disaffected and formed a chapter of another organization. The rest met for a time and then meetings and business were informally suspended, and but little has been said since and nothing done.

He goes on to say that up until the time of de facto dissolution, the Beta Chapter had enjoyed a superb reputation, but any chance of a revival appeared remote. Further, in view of his faculty colleagues' unfriendly attitude toward secret societies because of the activities of other organizations, he (Whitlock) was not in a position to lend his name to any effort to revive the Beta Chapter.

One wonders what would have happened if the Beta Chapter's founder and founding member of the Alpha Chapter, Hermann Merrills Johnson (1839), had remained at Ohio Wesleyan University. After six years in Ohio, he accepted a position in 1850 as professor of English at Dickinson College in Carlisle, Pennsylvania. He again began efforts to establish a chapter of the Eclectic Society on another campus. His efforts met with success, for on May 12, 1852, the Gamma Chapter of the Eclectic Society of Phi Nu Theta became active at Dickinson with three students as members. It was the first Greek letter fraternity at Dickinson. H. M. Johnson's success was short-lived. The Gamma Chapter fell victim to faculty hostility to fraternities; it was suppressed after a mere two months of existence. Dickinson's Web site in 2005 explained, "The faculty condemned any group that would not allow them immediate access at any time, and forced the organization to disband." It is ironic that the newly elected president of Dickinson just after the forced dissolution of the Gamma Chapter was Charles Collins (1837), one of the four founders—or perhaps, more precisely, "prefounders"—of Eclectic. In the account of his life on the Dickinson College 2005 Web site, this comment is offered: "The number of students enrolled in the College rose under his administration even though Collins himself was not widely popular with the student body. This was largely due to his response to independent student activities like secret fraternities and 'rough and tumble' football." Charles Collins's successor as president of Dickinson was none other than H. M. Johnson, who held that office from 1860 until his death in 1868. The effects of the Civil War and the financial woes of Dickinson occupied his attention during these years, and there is no indication he attempted to revive the Gamma Chapter when he succeeded his fraternity-unfriendly "frater in Eklektos" as president.

The last serious attempt to found another chapter of the Society was the previously discussed effort by Genesee College students in 1864 and again in 1865. Eclectic was wooed on several other occasions (notably by Delta Upsilon in June 1884) to join existing national fraternities as their Wesleyan chapter, but by the end of the 1860s, it was fairly well established as a policy that the Eclectic Society of Phi Nu Theta would remain a local fraternity, unique and dedicated to Wesleyan. Eclectic's flirtation with "going national" was at an end.

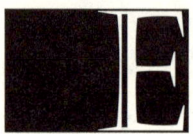ric North and Paul North Rice turned to Professor Morris Barker Crawford (1874) to draft the history of the 1870s. His is a more personal account, since he lived what he was writing. He contributed much to the writing of the history of the early years and was described by the joint authors as knowing more about the history of the fraternity than any other person living at the time that they were drafting the history, just prior to the Centennial celebration of 1937. He knew many of the founders and lived until 1940.

At the beginning of the 1870s, meetings of the Society were held in the building belonging to Meech & Stoddard on Main Street (which was torn down in 1929, to be replaced by a building for the W. T. Grant Company at 404 Main Street). According to the 1908 *Catalogue*, Eclectics moved into this building on Main Street in 1853, but the *Catalogue* appears to have been in error, for the minutes of the Society show that the Society occupied these rooms only from August 5, 1856. They left them to occupy the first clubhouse on College Place (later Wesleyan Place) in 1882.

According to records and photos, the Meech & Stoddard spaces (1856–82) comprised three rooms on the second floor of the building: a large front room where the regular meetings were held; a "good-sized" room at the rear, which was used for suppers and miscellaneous purposes; and a "fair-sized" room in between, into which opened the entrance door at the head of two flights of narrow stairs. This middle room served as a coat room, assembly room for initiates just before their initiation ceremony, charades play room, room for extra tables for supper at annual meetings, and so on. Discussion of the possibility of an Eclectic House must have begun by the beginning of the 1870s, for the Socratic Literary Society ("the Socrats" or "SLS") was formally chartered by Act of the General Assembly of the State of Connecticut on July 5, 1870. The alumni arm of Eclectic was formed to support the broad goals of the Fraternity, but more particularly to provide a means to acquire real property and build endowment funds. The incorporators were Brothers John M. Van Vleck (1850), George G. Reynolds (1841), Gilbert Haven (1846), William N. Rice (1865), Stephen H. Olin (1866), and Rhys B. Gwillim (1866).[1] The first Annual Meeting of the Socrats was held on July 17, 1872, and the custom existed from the beginning of electing all living members of the rising senior delegation to membership in the Socratic Literary Society.

The program of the regular meetings of Eclectic during the decade following 1870 was, except as noted below, much the same as it was when Professor Crawford wrote his description in the mid-1930s. Literary exercises consisted of two analyses of essays, two essays, and two criticisms of essays. Time was then allowed for criticism from any member present who felt so moved. An "extemporaneous review" of some article or book took the place of the so-called "special topic" of later days. Also usually included in regular meetings through the 1870s were two "declamations," a popular pastime and academic exercise of the day. Once a month, these regular exercises were replaced by a debate for which the question of debate and four debaters were appointed in advance. Following the formal debate, the question was thrown open to the floor, and the resulting discussions often became quite animated.

At that time the meetings were held on Friday evenings. As Professor Crawford phrased it, there was only one "appointment" for each college class on Saturday morning, and it was either a lecture or something which involved a minimum of preparation on the students' part. There was therefore no pressure of college work to interfere with attendance at the fraternity meeting or with prolonging the meetings, as the members might choose. Nor was there any such itch to get away over the weekend then, as the days of the automobile were still to come. Professor Crawford commented, however, that faithful attendance at the meetings and punctual fulfillment of appointments were more successfully maintained in the 1930s than in his years in college sixty years before.

After the regular meetings, many brothers remained to sing or otherwise amuse themselves. George Ingraham (1871), son of Richard Ingraham (1842), was a fine musician with an exceptionally good voice. Squeezing the best accompaniment he could out of an old melodion, which was part of the modest furnishings, he used to lead the assembled in rousing songs. Later, James Nixon (1875), with a powerful tenor voice, became the song leader. One of the most popular songs that he introduced was "The Patriotic Glee." The fraternity song "With Joyful Songs We Come" was set to this tune for the Quadrennial of 1875. Professor Crawford modestly omitted to state that he was the author of the words to this song, still popular with Eclectics in the 1950s. In the 1870s, there were practically no college songs. Professor Calvin S. Harrington's "Beside a Noble River's Tide" was in the old *Carmina Collegensia* (as well as in *The Wesleyan Song Book* of 1953) but was almost never sung. There were relatively few fraternity songs, and even those that existed—like S. H. Olin's (1866) "There's a Temple Grander, Lovelier," Professor William North Rice's (1865) "Phi Nu Theta Floreat," and Edward H. Rice's (1870) "'Tis Pleasant to Clasp the Warm Hand of a Brother"—were not sung with the frequency they were later. C. F. Rice's (1872) "Greeting from our Mystic Union" was as appropriate in the 1870s as it was later,[2] but it was not the custom to sing it to welcome Eclectic's "last adopted sons" in those earlier days. Surprisingly, there was no systematic effort to teach the freshman delegation fraternity songs.

Besides singing, the undergraduates would often amuse themselves with impromptu charades; on occasion, they would dance the Virginia reel. Professor Crawford commented that these terpsichorean enterprises were "much more merry than artistic."

Annual meetings were far smaller affairs than in later years, since there were fewer than thirty undergraduates and also fewer returning alumni. Refreshments served were far less elaborate, and the venue was usually confined to the rear room mentioned at the beginning of the chapter, with some expansion into the middle room, if necessary.

It is interesting to read in Professor Crawford's cover letter forwarding his draft of the Fraternity's history in the 1870s the following comment: "As to the later seventies, I am quite sure that I am correct as to the general fact that Eclectic slipped back from its best standards during that period." In supporting this assertion, he cites the fact that only one Eclectic was elected to Phi Beta Kappa from the class of 1880, and in the manuscript he points out the declining percentage of Eclectics elected to the prestigious scholarly honorary society—from 65 percent in the first five years to 42 percent in the second half of the decade. Professor Crawford had to admit that, during the latter half of the 1870s, Psi Upsilon, always Eclectic's rival, shone brighter.

In his manuscript, however, he does mention the names of several Eclectics whom he considered leading men of that period: G. Brown Goode (1870), who stayed on at Wesleyan to organize the collections comprising the Wesleyan Museum and then departed in 1877 to become director of the National Museum of the Smithsonian Institution in Washington, D.C.; Edgar M. Smith (1871), valedictorian of his class and, after a number of years in the Methodist church and education, became president of Illinois Wesleyan and then Carleton College in Missouri; Frank Mason North, Charles Francis Rice, Arthur Benton Sanford, and John Newton Holt, all of the class of 1872, referred to as an "admirable quartet" for maintaining the best traditions of the Fraternity and living extremely productive lives after college; Alfred Charles True (1873), a teacher of Latin and Greek at Wesleyan who became a key official of the U.S. Department of Agriculture's Office of Experiment Stations; and last William Ingraham Haven (1877), a leading Methodist and then general secretary of the American Bible Society.

In all fairness to the Eclectics of the 1870s, it should be pointed out that they succeeded the era of the reformers and giants of the 1860s— W. P. Hubbard, H. C. M. Ingraham, "Billy" Rice, S. H. Olin, W. O. Atwater, W. H. H. Phillips, and H. D. Harrower—an awe-inspiring group to follow. They also preceded another series of impressive delegations in the 1880s, when, according to Professor Crawford, "Eclectic rallied well to its proper position, not only in point of scholarship, but also in its participation in noncurricular activities, such as the *Argus*, the Glee Club, and the football and baseball teams."

CHAPTER 6

THE 1880S A HOUSE OF ONE'S OWN

P aul North Rice and his colleagues ceased their efforts on a manuscript history of the Society after covering the decade of the 1870s. The reader may note a change in style and approach as this author launches into unexplored and, quite frankly, challenging waters.

The minutes of September 17, 1880, indicate that about half the candidates proposed for election that year were rejected. There are clear indications that the "blackballing" (a term used in the minutes) was the result of a deep division in the House. The rejections are laid to the actions of one "party" against the other. Members evidently worked on at least a structural solution to the problem. A "Cultivating Committee" of members from three classes was appointed at the meeting of April 1, 1881. By 1883, the committee had considerable influence over the vetting of candidates. Elections of new members were conducted at special meetings of the Society in September 1883 with "notification at the discretion of the Cultivating Committee." Throughout the decade initiations were generally held shortly after election of members. Late September was the favored time for initiations—even of freshmen. There appears to have been no regular pledge period of three months or so as in later years, but the term "pledging" appears for the first time in the minutes of September 9, 1885, so the concept was alive at mid-decade. There is no mention as to the reason, but to the shock of the brothers, three candidates elected to membership in the fall of 1885 did not accept election. Reverse blackballing was evidently a new experience for the Society. Toward the end of the decade another event occurred which would not have been permitted under mid-twentieth-century rules. Cyrus D. Foss Jr. (1891), son of the former university president, was "given an election" on April 1, 1887, evidently as a subfreshman. He and other classmates who were elected in early September were initiated on September 30, 1887.

Singing played an increasingly important role in fraternity activities.

The Society voted in 1880 to sing every Saturday evening in the Alpha Club rooms, and it became the custom to sing a fraternity song before the literary exercises at regular meetings. The lack of formal musical indoctrination for new members was remedied by vote of the Society on September 20, 1889, when the Choragus was directed "to instruct the members elect in society songs."

The minutes of meetings throughout 1881 reflect a considerable amount of tension among the Eclectics of the time, continuing the ill feelings between two "parties" mentioned at the beginning of this chapter. There evidently had been incidents of hazing, for the minutes of September 23, 1881, record the abandonment of the "outdoor part" of the initiation (except the "silent walk") as well as "anything derogatory to the dignity of . . . and insulting to . . . the gentlemen being initiated." These abandoned exercises were later referred to as the "ceremonies at the graveyard" on initiation night. All outdoor portions of initiation activities were abolished concurrent with the initiation of September 25, 1885. The next year the term "sub rosa exercises" was first mentioned, probably replacing the less pleasant activities of previous years. The term "pledge" was also used, although the period between election and initiation continued to be about a week.

Relations between the fraternities and the college authorities were not smooth in the winter and spring term of 1881. At the regular meeting in Eclectic Hall of February 25, 1881, a committee was established to confer with the other societies concerning the president's "command" prohibiting suspended students from attending meetings of societies, if they remained in town. The president at the time was John Wesley Beach (1845), ironically an Eclectic, who had less than good relations with a number of constituencies.[1] A week later, the Society formally resolved that "The Faculty has no right to dictate what men the Society shall receive into its meetings." The matter was resolved the week after that; the minutes of the Society of March 11, 1881, state, "The Faculty had withdrawn the objectionable part of the decision."

The most serious indications of tension within the Fraternity appeared in minutes of the same month that witnessed the outrage at college policy on attendance at fraternity meetings. A committee was formed to discuss unacceptable behavior on the part of some brothers. Leo A. Bergholz (1882) was cited in particular. These members were accused of behavior "insulting the Society" on March 18, 1881. Again, a week later (March 25, 1881) the affair seems to have been resolved. Still, one can read between the lines that all was not well until a year or so later.

Specific indications that academics were reemphasized in the mid-1880s appear in society records. The maintenance of a file of examinations is first mentioned in minutes of April 24, 1884. The exams were to be maintained and preserved by class—1884 through 1887. A file of examinations was still being maintained as late as the late 1950s.

Bylaws of the Eclectic Society of Phi Nu Theta were revised in 1885. Among the provisions of the revision were: regular meetings were to be held on Friday "one-half hour after the ringing of the study bell"; membership should consist of no more than twenty-five active members; five honorary members could be elected; a quorum would consist of six members (not a very positive comment on attendance); and specifics on literary exercises were set forth (not differing very much from previous and subsequent practices). Reemphasizing the importance of scholarship, an assessment of five dollars was imposed first on seniors and then on juniors for the benefit of the library.

With the reemphasis on scholarship, the social aspects of fraternity life were not ignored. The Socratic Literary Society ("Socrats") raised funds for a "clubhouse." The alumni organization discussed various plans through the 1870s and actually purchased land on Cross Street, but further action materialized when the Building Committee of the Socrats purchased a lot on College Place (later Wesleyan Place) from Wesleyan University for the sum of $1,400. The transaction was recorded in the committee's report of June 22, 1880. A design for a building was approved which made provision for a "lodge room" on the second story; dining room for the Alpha Club, sitting room, and kitchen on the first; and housekeeper rooms in the basement. There were no provisions for student living quarters. The estimated cost for the building was $12,000. Approval was given at the Socratic Literary Society meeting of June 28, 1881, to sell the Cross Street lot, presumably to help finance the construction of the facility. Eclectic was the second fraternity to build a house for its own use, Psi Upsilon having constructed its first building on Broad Street, just north of Court Street, in 1878. The Eclectic House was presented with appropriate ceremony by the Socratic Literary Society to the Eclectic Society of Phi Nu Theta at the latter's Annual Meeting of June 27, 1882, held in its new quarters.

Although a source of great satisfaction to Eclectics, the acquisition of their own facility was not devoid of problems. Even before the Society occupied the building, there was concern for the security of "the lodge room." The minutes of May 12, 1882, record the need to ensure that the room be locked. In 1886, minutes of February 6 state, "The Eclectic Society disapproves of the use of its clubhouse by any of its members for private social entertainments or parties at which ladies or other nonmembers shall be present without the approval of the Society." Difficulties persisted to the end of the decade. Minutes of October 25, 1889, reflect the fact that material was being taken from the Meeting Room without authorization. Also mentioned a number of times in minutes after 1882 was the challenge of retaining matrons, for whom quarters had been built in the House. Several resigned in less than a year. No provision for athletic facilities had been included in the original design of the clubhouse, but that situation was remedied in November 1889, when the Socrats advanced funds for the construction of permanent tennis courts on the property. On a number of other occasions, the undergraduates appealed to the Socratic Literary Society for funds to help meet the increasing expenses of the new House. The Socrats responded as they could. As a related matter, "term taxes" on undergraduates, which supported the operation of the Fraternity, were set at $3.37 for upperclassmen and $2.10 for freshmen in for the spring term of 1881 and rose to $6.00 for all by the winter term of 1888.

Throughout the decade, literary exercises continued to be at the heart of weekly fraternity meetings. With two analyses, two essays, two criticisms, and two declamations due each week, the burden was fairly heavy on the active members, numbering about twenty-five in any given year. Freshmen appeared in literary appointments as soon as they were initiated. Nevertheless, meetings on Friday evenings were not extraordinarily long, averaging two to two and one-half hours. Attendance at meetings was not always stellar, and the minutes comment on that fact every now and again. The topics of essays varied broadly: political ("The Hayes Administration"), religious ("Itinerant System of the M. E. Church"), literary ("The Poetry of John Laxe"), biographical ("The Marquis de Lafayette"), college-related ("A Plea for a Wesleyan University

Marking System"), social issues ("Prohibition in Maine"), and burning issues of the times ("Negro and Women's Suffrage"). All these essays have been preserved in the Eclectic Repository, now in the possession of Wesleyan's Olin Library. They would make a fascinating source for research on the thinking and attitudes of undergraduates in the nineteenth and twentieth centuries, but that is another topic for another day.

The year 1887 marked the "semi-centennial" of the founding of Eclectic. Discussion of how the event should be celebrated began at the Annual Meeting of June 23, 1885. Professor W. N. Rice was appointed chair of the committee. A celebration was held on Tuesday, June 28 and Wednesday, June 29, 1887. On Tuesday, the Fraternity held a reception in the clubhouse from 3:30 to 7:30 p.m. followed by the Annual Meetings of both the Eclectic Society and the Socratic Literary Society. Public exercises followed the next day at 8:00 p.m. in the Methodist Church in town. The program consisted of an "opening concert by the Temple Quartette of Boston" (a vocal group); music by the Fraternity; a prayer; a "President's address" by Stephen Henry Olin; more music by the Fraternity; and an oration by the Rt. Rev. Bishop Cyrus David Foss, D.D., LL.D., before a final musical selection by the Boston singers. By all accounts, the exercises were very well received.

The decade of the 1880s was one of quiet growth and significant change. The building of the first Eclectic House testified to the aspect of change. The delegations of the decade witnessed the growth somewhat in numbers, but particularly in stature. Names such as James A. Develin (1883), contributor of note to the University; Edward B. VanVleck (1884), renowned mathematician and professor first at Wesleyan and then at the University of Wisconsin, son of "Uncle Johnny"; George S. Ingraham (1885) of the prominent Eclectic family; Frank D. and George D. Beattys (1885) as well as Harry H. Beattys (1888), members of another nineteenth-century Eclectic clan; Fred M. Davenport (1889), Progressive Republican, Member of Congress and stellar alumnus of both College and Fraternity; Ashley H. Thorndike (1889), distinguished professor of English at Columbia University; and many more. There were indeed giants in those days.

CHAPTER 7

ECLECTIC IN
THE 1890S

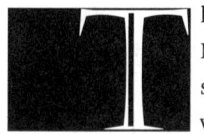his decade was a fairly quiet one for the Society. Minutes and other documents reflect few major issues or events. The relatively new clubhouse proved very popular, but inadequate to the number of members using the facility. Another significant problem was the lack of living quarters for upperclassmen, increasingly a feature of fraternity life at the end of the nineteenth century. The college actively discouraged living quarters in fraternities until the student body enrollment increased significantly (from 190 in 1887 to 327 ten years later),[1] and fraternities could help solve the housing problem. Psi Upsilon would lead the way in their new house constructed on High Street in 1893. From a personal point of view, a facet of this decade is the appearance of names of brothers being initiated over 100 years ago whom I knew personally in the mid- to late 1950s. It brings home that we 1959ers are certified senior citizens in this year of grace 2006.

Over the space of six days in September, 1890, fourteen members of the class of 1894 were elected to membership, but only five were initiated on October 10. Evidently there was some unpleasantness at the initiation, for a special meeting called on October 14 voted on disapproval of some sophomore behavior toward initiate William L. Snow (1894). It appears that quasi-hazing was a lingering problem in the new decade. During the same academic year, on March 20, 1891, the Society elected Edward L. Thorndike (1895) and three others to membership. E. L. Thorndike distinguished himself as a leading American psychologist and professor of psychology at Columbia University, joining his brother A. H. Thorndike (1889) as the first of another multigenerational Eclectic clan. The younger Thorndike was initiated on October 2, 1891, along with Henry Ingraham Harriman (1895) and eight others. Brother Harriman's name is well known to generations of Wesleyan graduates as the lead donor in 1926 of Harriman Hall, named in memory of his father, Daniel Gould Harriman (1864), also an Eclectic.

Singing continued to play a significant role in house activities. The Society voted on May 15, 1891, to rehearse and sing its songs at least twice a week under the direction of the Choragus. The next year H. Loren Clements (1896) was elected to membership at a meeting on February 3, 1892, evidently as a subfreshman. Brother Clements along with his delegation mate John A. Anderson later served on the committee which produced "The Songs of Phi Nu Theta" for the Centennial of the University in 1931 and was very involved in musical activities during his undergraduate years. He wrote the music to two of the songs included in the Eclectic collection ("Fraternity Ode" and "Reunion Song"). He returned to the campus for his sixtieth reunion in 1956, and this author was assigned to the committee of the House to welcome him and see to any needs he might have. He regaled us with stories of his years at college and particularly of the musical life, which was vigorous and popular.

The year 1892 also witness the demise of the successor to the Quadrennial exercises, discussed in chapter 4. The exercises had been renamed "Quinquecennial" in view of the admittance of a fifth fraternity to the rotation. A committee was formed to discuss the Quinquecennial with Psi Upsilon, and both fraternities were in favor of abolishing it per the minutes of the Society of March 14, 1892, and confirmed by vote of the Annual Meeting of June 28, 1892.

Literary exercises were modified slightly per minutes of a meeting on February 10, 1893. "News of the Week" replaced informal talks on various subjects. The experiment lasted a little more than four years. Reinstated debates on a monthly basis (dropped in May 1894) replaced "News of the Week" in April 1897.[2] Another slight modification had occurred a year earlier when the number of declamations became optional at one or the traditional two per meeting. The system of requiring essays to be submitted on society paper established in the mid-1860s was flouted on occasion throughout the decade. The minutes note this transgression on the part of literary appointees several times, but reflect the allowance of the period of a week between reading in meeting and formal acceptance for preservation in the Eclectic Repository. Topics covered in essays varied considerably: literary criticism, poetry, domestic politics, international relations, personal experiences, and burning issues of the day, such as Darwinism versus religion, popular election of the president, and "Negro disenfranchisement." For the first time at the end of the decade the minutes (November 24, 1899) reflect the consideration of "stories" as an appropriate part of the "literary bulletin." A committee was appointed to look into the matter and also to consider how declamations might be improved.

Inflation and other factors, such as the cost of upkeep of facilities, affected the financial situation of the House during the 1890s. The term tax rose from six dollars at the beginning of the decade to ten dollars at its end, and some members evidently found the tax steep. There was a motion on December 3, 1899, to amend the bylaws to require payment of interest on overdue tax payments at the rate of 2 percent per month. The motion did not carry, but the fact that it was put forward is sure indication of a problem.

Membership increased during the decade, paralleling the growth of the University. Five freshmen were initiated on October 10, 1890, and ten on October 2, 1891. This latter number remained fairly constant for freshman initiates during the rest of the decade. Of course, an occasional upperclassman joined the House in most years. The increase in membership put pressure on the College Place house. As early as October 1896, there was undergraduate "grumbling" about the inferiority of the Eclectic house to those of Psi Upsilon and Delta Kappa Epsilon.[3] In an expression of sentiment of May 26, 1899, the undergraduates advised the Socrats that it was their preference that a new clubhouse be built, but if that proved to be impossible, a remodeling and expansion of the seventeen-year-old existing House would be an acceptable alternative. The resolution of this situation will be a major topic in the next chapter.

The Eclectic Key. Badge of the Fraternity, worn on a key chain by members. Miniature pins could be worn by wives, fiancées, girlfriends, and sisters.

Eclectic House in spring.
Designed by Henry Bacon of Lincoln Memorial fame and completed in 1907.

Eclectic House in fall.
The flat roof caused problems almost from the beginning.

Charles Collins (1837).
A prefounder of the Fraternity,
not formally initiated until 1852.
He served as president of Dickinson
College 1852–60. Photo
courtesy of Dickinson College.

Hermann M. Johnson (1839).
Founder of both the Beta and
Gamma Chapters and successor
to Charles Collins as president of
Dickinson College 1860–68.
Photo courtesy of Dickinson College.

Eric M. North (1909). Began a history of Eclectic for the centennial celebration of 1937 but was obliged to cease work due to press of duties as general secretary of the American Bible Society.

Paul N. Rice (1910). Continued the history of Eclectic through the 1860s. Wesleyan librarian 1953–56.

Morris B. Crawford (1874). Contributed a chapter on the 1870 toward the manuscript history for the centennial of 1937. Grand old man of Eclectic following the death of William N. Rice in 1928 until his own death in 1940.

First meeting places. All three rental locations were on the east side of Main Street and were occupied (left to right) 1846–51, 1851–56, and 1856–82, respectively.

First house. Served as Eclectic's own first clubhouse on College Place, 1882–1907. There were no accommodations for undergraduates, an increasingly sore point as time went on.

George G. Reynolds (1841).
The principal donor to the building
of the house at 200 High Street. His
portrait occupied the place of honor
over the fireplace for many years.

Joseph Cummings (1840).
Fifth president of Wesleyan
(1857–75) and the first of four
Eclectics to hold that office.

Cyrus D. Foss (1854).
Sixth president of Wesleyan
(1875–80) and the second Eclectic.

John W. Beach (1845).
Seventh president of Wesleyan
(1880–87) and the third Eclectic.

Edwin D. Etherington (1948).
Twelfth president of Wesleyan
(1967–70) and the fourth Eclectic.

he Civil War had a great effect on Eclectic, as pre-
viously discussed; the Spanish-American War, just
before the turn of the century, less so. There are
a number of reasons for this. The war was much
shorter (Secretary of State John M. Hay characterized it as "a splendid
little war"); it caused far fewer casualties on both sides; and its results
produced far less national trauma. Eclectic men served in the war, but
much less was made of their service than was made of that of their elder
and younger brothers-in-arms. An exception is highlighted in a letter
of William North Rice (1865) to his son, Edward L. Rice (1892), dated
April 1, 1899. Billy relates reports concerning Brother Charles R. Blundell (1891), a physician serving in Florida in the Army Medical Corps.
Other medical officers reportedly went into town "bumming" (i.e., ca-
rousing), leaving the men under their care to suffer—mainly from ma-
laria and yellow fever, but surgeon Blundell was a "model . . . a pattern
of conscientiousness and self-sacrifice." He stayed behind to minister
to the sick . . . and even gave up his quarters to house the wounded
and diseased. The events were mentioned in the address of G. "Row-
ley" Munroe (1893) at the annual Eclectic banquet in March 1899, and
Billy commented that they were "told beautifully . . . and touching[ly]."

The purist reader may object that the Spanish-American War belongs to the last decade of the nineteenth century, and that is true. In a
larger sense, however, the war marked the United States' entry onto the
world stage as a great power—and the history of that role belongs to the
twentieth century. Events in the Eclectic Society of Phi Nu Theta in the
last two or three years of the nineteenth century also presage developments in the next century. Chief among these was the development of
plans for and the construction of a fraternity house that would include
living quarters for undergraduates. The minutes of the Annual Meeting of the Socratic Literary Society, the alumni organization specifically

chartered to undertake capital projects, discussed a plan in 1898 to expand the existing clubhouse to include undergraduate living quarters, but the next year, the minutes of the Socrats' Annual Meeting (June 27, 1899) record that the plan was withdrawn and a committee appointed to look into the construction of a new house in a different location. To accommodate undergraduate desires for living accommodations, the Board of Directors (an executive committee composed of resident Socrats) was authorized to lease a "dormitory structure" for their use for the academic year 1899–1900 and for five years thereafter. The structure was a house at 246 High Street. The Socrats' minutes make no mention of the actual location, but the undergraduate minutes of the Regular Meeting on May 13, 1904, refer to the residence house at that address and to the fact that brothers would have to pay past bills before they could select a room for the next academic year. Three years earlier rules for the "dormitory" had been adopted[1] and provision made for room rent to be on the same basis as the term tax.[2]

The seven years from 1900 to 1907 witnessed the complicated process of authorization (Socrats' Annual Meeting of June 26, 1900), financing and fund-raising, groundbreaking (June 27, 1906), laying of the cornerstone (November 5, 1906), first use of the new Eclectic House at 200 High Street at the Annual Meetings held consecutively (as was the custom) on June 25, 1907, and formal dedication of the new facility on October 11, 1907. The cost associated with the new edifice was initially estimated to be $30,000, to be raised by subscription; but by 1903 the estimated cost had risen to $50,000;[3] and by completion of the building in 1907, the chairman of the Socrats' Building Committee, H. C. M. Ingraham, gave the total cost as about $20,000 for the land and $40,000 for the building.[4] After initially flirting with the idea of purchasing the Connecticut State Building from the recently concluded St. Louis Louisiana Purchase Centenary Exposition, disassembling it, and moving it to Middletown, the Building Committee of the Socrats—at the urging of member Stephen H. Olin—decided to engage architect Henry Bacon of New York City.[5] His sketches and floor plans, presented to a special Socratic Literary Society meeting in New York City on February 16, 1906, were accepted. Thus the future architect (selected 1912) of the Lincoln Memorial in Washington, D.C. (dedicated 1922), was able to "practice" on the Eclectic House—or at least we used to think so in the 1950s.

There's no denying certain similarities. Wesleyan Historian Dave Potts had more to add:

> This building was the first step toward bringing a highly distinguished American architect to serve as de facto campus planner and architect for Wesleyan from 1912 to his death in 1924. Bacon created Wesleyan's first campus plan (1913), and was the architect for: the swimming pool addition to Fayerweather (1914 [-2005]), Skull and Serpent (1914), Van Vleck Observatory (1915), Clark Hall (1916), Memorial Chapel renovation (1916), South College cupola/belfry (1919), and the initial design for Olin Library (1923). The last-mentioned was closely followed by McKim, Mead, and White in its final design. In 1923, Bacon won the highest award in his profession. Wesleyan's campus has by far the largest assemblage of his works, starting with Eclectic.[6]

The grand structure that stands at 200 High Street was inaugurated with much ceremony. Ground was broken by Judge George G. Reynolds (1841), the major contributor to the cost of the new house, at 9:00 a.m. on June 26, 1906, with subsequent spade turns by significant contributors of time, talent, and money: H. C. M. Ingraham (1864), C. D. Foss (1854), W. N. Rice (1865), R. S. Douglass (1861), J. M. Van Vleck (1850), C. H. Buck (1864), S. H. Olin (1866), W. P. Hubbard (1863), F. D. Beattys (1885), G. D. Beattys (1885), and A. E. Sutherland (1885). The participants, both graduates and undergraduates, then sang several Eclectic songs.[7]

The cornerstone was laid four months later, on November 5, 1906, at 4:15 p.m. Billy North Rice spoke and his remarks are fully recorded in the Eclectic Society minutes of that date. Among other things, he commented, "Buildings do not make the organization. It takes its character from the lives of its members." The following documents were placed in the cornerstone: a copy of the Charter of the Socratic Literary Society; a list of the members living and deceased of the Eclectic Society; a copy of the 1865 *Catalogue of Phi Nu Theta*; a copy of the Wesleyan *Argus* for October 17, 1906, containing a description of the building; a copy of the *Catalogue of Wesleyan University* for 1905–6; a copy of the *Penny Press* of Middletown for November 3, 1906; and a copy of the *Hartford Courant* for November 5, 1906. Brother John M. Van Vleck (1850) then laid the cornerstone with a new trowel and mallet, following which he addressed the crowd (full text in Society minutes). The exercises concluded with the singing of "Tela Mystica."[8]

The first formal use of the new house was for the Annual Meetings on June 25, 1907. At the Socrats' meeting, it was announced to the seventy in attendance that Mrs. S. H. Olin was donating a piano to the House and that her husband was donating two classical busts.[9] Additionally, H. C. M. Ingraham (1864) was donating a portrait of Judge Reynolds (1841) to be hung over the fireplace to honor the man who had done so much to make the new Eclectic House a reality[10] and who was the oldest living alumnus at the time, a contemporary of the founders, if not formally counted in that select company.

This meeting of the Socratic Literary Society, the owner of the House, set the terms under which the Eclectic Society of Phi Nu Theta could use the premises:

1. The Socrats would charge the undergraduate Society $10 per term ($30 a year) rent per man;
2. The total charge for rent of the rooms to the Society was $1,200 per year;
3. No more than eighteen residents were to be permitted to occupy rooms;
4. The Alpha Club (dining club) would pay the Socrats $75 per month for help, the Socrats agreeing to make up the balance of expenses (ca. $30 per month) out of Socratic funds.

The Meeting set the formal dedication of the House for the next fall.[11]

The dedication occurred on Friday, October 11, 1907, in conjunction with initiation of new Eclectic members and the noting of the seventieth anniversary of the founding. Brother Van Vleck presided. He introduced the speakers: Judge G. G. Reynolds, who spoke on college fraternities in general and Eclectic in particular; H. C. M. Ingraham, chairman of the Building Committee, who addressed the architecture of the House and its hearkening back to the glories and simplicity of ancient Greece; and finally S. H. Olin, who paid tribute to the previous two speakers in ringing words and then to loud applause unveiled the portrait of George Greenwood Reynolds donated by Henry C. M. Ingraham.[12]

At the beginning of the decade the term tax was $10, and at the end, $17. The 70 percent increase undoubtedly resulted not only from additional expenses of the new House but also from other factors, such as inflation. Taste in periodicals did not differ much from previous years. Subscriptions for the year 1899–1900 included *Life*, *Century*, *Scribner's*, *American*, *London Illustrated News*, and *Review of Reviews*. Again at the beginning of the decade, the idea of "stories" as a suitable part of literary exercises was raised as a topic at a regular meeting and referred to a committee, which never formally reported back to the meeting.[13] The time for such ventures had not yet come. The issue of coeducation at Wesleyan was a hot topic. Brother Seward V. Coffin (1889) reported to the undergraduates in a March 1900 meeting concerning the activities of the Young Alumni Association of New York.[14] The minutes do not give much insight into the discussions, other than that they were vigorous, but David Potts's history of these years makes clear that the New York Group and Brother Coffin were strongly anti-coeducation.[15] The undergraduates may have trodden lightly in this area because a number of influential Socrats were pro-coeducation, including John M. Van Vleck and William North Rice.

The minutes of March 30, 1900, mention that a junior class "bum" was to be held during the spring term and that the freshman delegation was to provide entertainment. The term had been used at least as early as 1890 in connection with both the senior and junior delegations, although not with much detail as to what was involved. The term was certainly one of opprobrium when used describing the activities of physicians with less dedication than Brother Charles R. Blundell (1891) described at the beginning of this chapter, but not so with undergraduate activities in the spring of 1900. More light is shed in a memorandum from Noel E. Bensinger (1914) to Eric M. North (1909) concerning his undergraduate experiences 1910–14 and in response to Brother North's plea for anecdotes for the projected history of Eclectic for the centenary. Brother Bensinger wrote in the 1930s:

> During the years 1910 to 1914 when I was an undergraduate, each
> delegation would have its so-called "Bum" once a year to which
> the rest of the fraternity was, as a rule, invited. A "Bum" was an
> informal get-together with wrestling matches, boxing and various

kinds of good-natured horse-play and games, winding up with a spread of some kind in the dining room and seasoned with short speeches, mostly of the impromptu variety. Whether these "Bums" are still part of fraternity life, I do not know. They added much to the good-fellowship of our life together.[16]

"Bums" had disappeared by the 1950s, but an echo remained in the annual informal Christmas party, when brothers would let down their hair and exchange jibes and token gifts that were not always in the most delicate of taste.

Officers of the Fraternity in this decade were as they had been since the 1860s and would be fifty years later—with one notable exception. There was an undergraduate janitor who was paid two dollars a week by the Socrats. By the 1950s the office had become paid staff and not an undergraduate office. In the minutes of October 3, 1902, it was moved and approved that there be no "finger snapping" at the regular initiation that occurred a week later. "Finger snapping" or "a round of clicks" was the approved ("cool") manner of expressing approval in the 1950s. Something had to be really fantastic to gain a round of regular applause. I can remember a Wesleyan Series concert by a prima donna of the era, Rita Streich, dressed in a ravishing red gown, who was roundly applauded—undoubtedly for her marvelous recital, but also for the packaging. It was a real mark of distinction in Eclectic Hall to have a round of applause instead of the usual clicks following the presentation of a literary exercise. It may have happened once or twice a year during my undergraduate years 1955–59.[17]

The year 1903 also saw the approval of a new Constitution and By-laws Book, with only slight changes to earlier provisions. Also, only one debate per term would form part of literary exercises. On the lighter side, a spring launch ride would again provide a bit of diversion for the undergraduates. The rides were evidently popular in this decade. The Annual Meeting held on June 23, 1903, was attended by Willard M. Rice (1837), the last of the founders who shortly before had written down his recollections of the origins of Phi Nu Theta, quoted extensively in chapter 1. It would be his last attendance, for he died on March 6, 1904, just short of his eighty-seventh birthday. With the death of George Landon (1841) at age eighty-seven in June 1904, Judge George G. Reynolds of the same class became the oldest living member of the Society, an honor that he retained for close to nine years.

Rules for freshmen changed at the beginning of 1903–4. At the recommendation of the Chairmen of the Cultivation Committees of the various fraternities and by vote of the House on October 12, 1903, freshmen were obliged to wear a pledge button until initiated. There is no mention of the freshman cap that later bedeviled new undergraduates. The etiquette of the use of the fraternity key and its associated pin was spelled out by provision of the bylaws approved at a Regular Meeting on October 23 of the same year: no fraternity key or pin should be given to any persons except sisters (!), wives, or fiancées of members. The academic year ended on a high note when it was announced at the Annual Meeting that Brother Paul Nixon (1904) had been awarded a Rhodes Scholarship from Connecticut, the first Wesleyan graduate to be so honored. As a matter of interest, of the eleven Rhodes Scholars that Wesleyan boasted from 1904 to 1970, three were Eclectics: Paul Nixon (1904), Parker Newhall (1915), and Alan J. Gayer (1964).

In earlier years, pledging of subfreshman seems to have been fairly common. By 1906, however, feeling turned against the practice. Minutes from the regular meeting of the Society on February 17, 1906, indicate that it was the sentiment of the Fraternity that all pledging of subfreshmen be postponed until the fall—and that it be agreed to by all the fraternities. As in later years, the problem of controlling the use of a telephone for general use arose. The first mention of the installation of a telephone appeared at the very end of 1904.[18] The telephone was to be installed in the "dormitory" at 246 High Street, but the motion did not carry. By the end of January 1905, however, opinion had shifted and an instrument was approved for installation at a cost of thirty dollars per year.[19] Fourteen months later, the telephone was to be moved from the "dormitory" to the clubhouse on College Place with indications that unpaid long distance bills were a problem.[20] The year 1906 also marked the initiation on October 12 of the Delegation of 1910, including Paul North Rice, whose efforts led to the beginning of this history.

As the Society prepared to move into its new clubhouse, the dignity of proceedings at meetings seemed to be on the undergraduates' minds. By a motion passed on March 8, 1907, it was established that the Proedros, the senior presiding over the meeting and dining hall for the week, would wear an academic gown at regular meetings. After several false starts, creative writing finally found a place in literary exercises. The new form of the exercises for the next meeting, approved by the Regular Meeting on May 17, 1907, included a short story in essay form; a short talk; two declamations, judged by members; and a debate. Regular analyses and essays were to resume thereafter. Essays, however, could be creative writing, as shown by their appearance—along with more traditional forms—in the list of appointments from then on.

Decorum was a concern in the new House: "No fellow will come down to supper or to Sunday noon meal without collars" (i.e., with shirt, coat, etc.—and not sweaters).[21] History was also of interest. At the Annual Meeting on June 23, 1908, Brother Charles Reynolds (1882) of Middletown presented the doors of the old meeting room on Main Street to the Society, noting that Brother George N. Phelps (1864) and his father had manufactured the doors. It is unclear what happened to this relic of the past, but the doors to Eclectic Hall in the 1950s appeared different from the general construction of the rest of the House. I suspect they were these very same doors, modified to accommodate the changed location.

Academic year 1908–9 witnessed some tribulations for the Society. Minutes for the beginning of the year mention many overdue essays and presentations. Absenteeism at meetings seemed to be on the increase, and censure of members without valid excuses was threatened and sometimes imposed. The attractiveness of the new clubhouse caused it to be requested for many external functions, sometimes to the discomfort of the residents. Permission was sought from the Socrats for an increasing number of house parties. Minutes of March 5, 1909, indicate that the alumni organization took a dim view of such extravagance.

On the brighter side, a new Eclectic Song Book put together by H. Loren Clements (1896) and others was completed by the beginning of 1909, and a new custom was begun which lasted at least for the next fifty years or so. At the Annual Meeting of June 28, 1910, Eric M. North for the Delegation of 1909 presented nameplates for the residential rooms in the new House with the names of each occupant engraved upon them. When the Delegation of 1959 graduated, the plates were still being maintained with their history of room occupants.

CHAPTER 9

THE 1910S

THE GREAT WAR

T he public phone in the new House continued to be a problem. Minutes of the September 30, 1910, meeting mention the Thesaurophylax's unenviable task of chasing down long distance calls for billing purposes. Eleven freshmen, a relatively large number, were initiated into the Fraternity on October 7, 1910. Literary exercises at initiation included:

1 Analysis (vice 2) of an essay entitled "Unconscious Socialistic Tendencies in the U.S."
2 Essays entitled "Woodrow Wilson, a Modern Reformer" and "Witchcraft in Salem"
1 Declamation, "Grattan's Invective Against Carey"
1 Reading of a story entitled "Horo Ruby Played"

A special meeting of the Society was called three days later because of a report of misconduct by four sophomores in hazing certain freshmen. The miscreants were censured.[1] Hazing was not a traditional part of Eclectic life, although freshmen did have certain obligations both before and after initiation. Whenever matters got out of hand, as they did on a few occasions, balance was soon restored.

One of the 1910 initiates was Noel E. Bensinger (1914), who was quoted concerning the custom of delegation "Bums" in the previous chapter. His further observations on his college years (1910–14) are well worth quoting in full:

For some years before my time, I believe, and during my first two years, there existed within the undergraduate society a "secret order" known as B.L.G. (Bare Legged Goddess). The sophomore delegation each year was initiated into B.L.G. by the juniors and seniors, and this initiation made up seven-fold for the absence of roughhousing in our regular fraternity initiation. It was designed to take the "cockiness" out of the sophomore delegation and was effective at least for the evening of the initiation, which was held in the late fall of the year, as I recall it.

When our delegation became juniors, we refused to initiate the sophomores, and B.L.G. died a natural death, so far as I know. Its ideals, if any, and its shrine were not exactly in harmony with the Eclectic tradition. It was mostly a vent for animal spirits.

I think it fair to say that the central interest of the Society in my period was in scholarship, though certainly not to the exclusion of athletics and other extra-curricular interests. Five of my own delegation were elected to Phi Beta Kappa. During at least three of my four years, Eclectic was well represented on athletic teams and in college offices, and the Fraternity was always well regarded all over the campus. Our relations with Alpha Delta Phi and Chi Psi were especially cordial in the 1910–14 period.

The influence of Eclectic was always for clean fraternity "politics" and against "deals" with other houses in college elections. We always had the feeling that the college faculty and administrative officers looked upon the Eclectic Society as representing the best in the fraternity life of the college.[2]

Brother Bensinger's comments reflect the ideals that still resonated with graduates and undergraduates more than forty years after the period he described.

The fall term tax in 1910 was seventeen dollars, according to minutes of October 10, 1910. Secrecy was still very much the rule concerning what went on at meetings, but evidently there had been breaches. Brothers at the meeting of November 2, 1910, were strictly admonished to remember that the proceedings of the Society were secret. A custom of the time that had echoes in the 1950s concerned the "customary 24 hours' silence" to be observed with initiates;[3] by 1955 the time was reduced to six hours or so.

Cultural changes in society affected the life of the fraternity. Smoking was becoming more accepted, and there was earlier reference to smoking in the parlor at certain times being acceptable, but the minutes of November 21, 1910, indicate that indiscriminate smoking about the House was not permitted, especially during the Sunday night sings.[4]

Another such matter was the consumption of alcoholic beverages. The Methodist background of both Wesleyan and Eclectic carried with it a strong tradition of abstinence, if not prohibitionism. The Eighteenth Amendment to the U.S. Constitution banning the manufacture, sale, or transportation of intoxicating liquors did not enter into force until 1920, so during this decade, federal law did not apply. House rules (and state law) did, however, and the introduction of alcoholic beverages was prohibited by several resolutions passed in 1913–14. Two brothers were censured for violating the rule, and a further expression of sentiment was approved that no brother should come into the House drunk.[5] This and other matters of deportment were acted upon by the Socrats at their Annual Meeting of June 19, 1916. The alumni body (including the soon-to-graduate senior class), legal owners of the House, unanimously adopted a resolution concerning the House:

No card-playing on Sunday
No gambling
No introduction of alcoholic beverages
Infractions must be reported by Eclectic members to the Socrats' Board of Directors (resident alumni).[6]

The undergraduates further codified a strict provision concerning alcohol, drunkenness, and censure in a Bylaw approved May 28, 1918. House parties were also a concern to the older generation. Resident alumni of a number of fraternities met at William North Rice's house in June 1913 and agreed that "house parties are a nuisance." There was considerable discussion as to whether they should be limited to one per year or abolished altogether. No general solution emerged, but in the case of Eclectic, the matter was referred to the Board of Directors "with power."[7] No formal action ensued, and the undergraduates evidently trod somewhat softly, seeking permission from the leading members of the Board of Directors before scheduling house parties.

A surprising issue resurfaced in the spring of 1914. Phi Nu Theta received a letter from the Kappa Phi fraternity of Cornell proposing that there be an amalgamation of several local fraternities to form a national fraternity. After minimal discussion, the Society refused the offer and directed the Epistoleus to write Kappa Phi to that effect. Eclectic would remain a Wesleyan fraternity.[8]

In the summer of the same year, William North Rice, on behalf of the Board of Directors, sent a letter to Henry Bacon, architect of the clubhouse. In it Billy cites a problem with leaks in the roof and asks the assistance of a Mr. Lincoln, an associate of Mr. Bacon, during his forthcoming visit to Middletown to discuss the Van Vleck observatory. Billy also asks Bacon's advice on the vines that were fast covering the front of the building.[9] Bacon responded that he thought that the vines added to the beauty of the Eclectic Society building and should not be removed, but he recommended that they not be allowed to cover any more of the structure. The meeting with Lincoln had already been scheduled in the meanwhile and was confirmed in the letter.[10] Leaks continued to be an occasional nuisance in the 1950s; flat roofs do tend to leak.

By December 1914, allusions to the war in Europe, raging since August, began to appear in society records. An analysis of an essay entitled "Submarine Warfare" appeared in the literary appointments,[11] and similar topics appeared with increasing frequency in the next three years. When the United States declared war on Germany and her allies in April 1917, life on campus changed radically. The following measures to support the war effort are included in Carl F. Price's succinct summary of the Great War's effects on Wesleyan:[12] the faculty granted leave of absence, with full credit for the year, to students desiring to enlist in army, navy, YMCA, or ambulance work, and 83 students (out of 376) immediately signed up to serve; almost every remaining student enrolled in the Reserve Officer Training Corps (ROTC) unit established on campus that same month; minor sports, dramatics, and dances were dropped; students wore army uniforms and drilled daily; a trench seamed part of the back campus, and armed guards challenged all comers; Clark Hall was closed and chapel exercises were suspended to save coal; the president of the University, William A. Shanklin, left for six months' service in YMCA uniform in France (Billy Rice served again as acting president in his absence); the ROTC unit was replaced by a Student Army Training Corps (SATC) in October 1918, and 270 students out of a total of 409 in college were inducted into it; college dormitories became barracks; a mess hall to serve 500 was erected on Wyllys Avenue; and the flu epidemic of 1918 claimed the lives of six students and one faculty member. The idea of Wesleyan as a military training establishment will undoubtedly shock readers who are unacquainted with the history of the College in the two world wars, but times were different then. Even the nation's commander-in-chief during World War I had a Wesleyan and Eclectic connection. Woodrow Wilson was a popular Wesleyan professor from 1888 to 1890 and had lived in a house on the site of the new Eclectic House.[13] According to the roster included in the Service of Commemoration on June 22, 1919, twenty-five Wesleyan men gave their lives in the Great War.[14] Of these, one was an Eclectic, Fred Henry Pillsbury (1900n), cited in the *Wesleyan University Bulletin* of May 1919 as the first Wesleyan man to lose his life in the war.

World War I's effect on the Fraternity was equally traumatic. The Board of Directors, with Billy Rice as a spokesman, gave a report to the Annual Meeting of the Socratic Literary Society on June 23, 1919. The report made the following points: Wesleyan began the year 1918–19 as a college, converted into a military school, and then reverted in the second term to a college; Phi Nu Theta started the year with only nine undergraduates, although during the year it initiated the unprecedented number of fifteen into the Fraternity; all except the physically unfit were mustered into the SATC upon its formation in October 1918 and were obliged to move into barracks; only six brothers remained in the House; the influenza epidemic caused the campus dining hall to close and be turned into an infirmary, and consequently a large number of nonmember students boarded at Eclectic; the completion of the military mess hall forced the closing of boarding operations in the House and the discharging of the matron, Miss Susan E. Clark, a popular employee of fifteen years' standing. Then came the armistice and a return to "normalcy" at the beginning of the second term. By the winter term, the House was full—in fact, overcrowded. The Alpha Club, the fraternity dining club, reopened but was obliged to take in Chi Psi members to help make ends meet. The former matron, Miss Clark, was asked to resume her post, but her health prevented her return. Reading the minutes, one gets the impression that the dislocation was at least a factor in her failing health, and both Socrats and undergraduates felt upset by the whole roller-coaster turn of events.

Literary exercises continued during the roller-coaster year, but at a reduced volume for brothers who were SATC members. They fulfilled their obligation by giving three-minute talks.[15] Special talks then became a regular part of exercises when things returned to normal, and their nature was prescribed by vote of the House: they were to be controversial in nature; to be assigned by the Epistoleus two days in advance of their presentation; and, if unsatisfactory, to be given again at the next meeting.[16] Earlier it had been decided that "no essay used or to be used in a course of the College be submitted in the literary program of this Society."[17] The relaxation of rules that evidently accompanied the dislocation of the war years no longer applied. Meetings in January 1919 saw a renewed set of standards voted: brothers were to wear suit and shoes (!) to meetings, collars at supper, and the fraternity key at all times while at college. A change campuswide to fraternity meeting night was adopted by Eclectic at the Regular Meeting of February 10, 1919. Henceforth such meetings would be held on Wednesday instead of Friday evenings. Although the reason for this change was not stated at the meeting, earlier references to the choice of meeting nights indicated that the advent of the automobile on campus in increasing numbers gave undergraduates far more freedom of motion. Friday nights could increasingly be given over to pursuits other than fraternity meetings.

The decade was most significantly marked by the effect of World War I on the College and the Fraternity, but other trends are noteworthy. The Fraternity lost a number of its stalwart alumni, dating back nearly to its founding, most notably H. C. M. Ingraham (1864) in February 1911, John M. Van Vleck (1850) in November 1912, and George G. Reynolds (1841) in January 1913. Judge Reynolds was able to attend the celebration of the seventy-fifth anniversary of the fraternity in the fall of 1912 and to address the assembled brothers for the last time. Customs associated with Eclectic Hall, which were still were observed in the 1950s, were documented for the first time in this decade. The term "Goat Room," referring to the Hall, appeared for the first time in 1911[18] and was repeated the next year in an admonition to the brothers to take better care of the Hall.[19] It was voted at the meeting of November 12, 1912, that all stand when the Proedros enters the Hall and that he enter last—and that a song be sung. Eleven months later, the custom of a walk-around downstairs with song, ending in the Hall, was initiated.[20] This custom was still observed forty-five years later. Last, brothers were urged to be more "sociable" when visitors came to the house.[21] I remember almost the same words emanating from the Epistoleus, Spud

Parker, in 1955 when he castigated members who sometimes acted less than warmly toward visitors. *Plus ça change, plus c'est la même chose.*

All was not solemn and serious in the second decade of the twentieth century. For example, the minutes of the Regular Meeting of May 8, 1912, report a lively debate on whether the House should buy "slippery" or "stiff" toilet paper. Brother John P. Maynard (1913) [father John W. (1883); son John W. (1945)] delivered an impassioned argument which "took the house by storm." The result was a unanimous vote passed for "the slippery kind." [22] One wonders what kind of a slick argument would produce such a resounding result.

By 1920 the new clubhouse was thirteen years old; the wear and tear was beginning to show. Additionally, the expenses of operating such a large structure were greater than expected. The final mortgage payment had been made in time for a ceremonial burning of the last mortgage note for $20,000 at the Socrats' Annual Meeting on June 23, 1919. There were even some extra funds available in unpaid subscriptions. It was decided in principle at the same meeting to apply these monies to an endowment fund. The Socrats' minutes for June 18, 1920, reflect an estimate of significant funds that would be required to make needed repairs and upkeep. The minutes also express the need to raise the amount charged to undergraduates for board and general use of the House.

By the spring of 1921, the cost of house operations put the Socrats more than $1,500 in debt. Billy North Rice, the chairman of the Socrats' Board of Directors, wrote about the problem to his son, Edward L. Rice, with more than a little candor:

> We are trying to arrange for a meeting of the Socratic Directors to consider what we are going to do with a deficit of $1,500 and a house that needs a lot of costly repairs. I wish those New York men had not forced us into the building of a house so enormously costly to build and to maintain; and I do not greatly value the pre-eminence of having the largest and finest dance-hall of all the college houses. Our enormously costly house tends to make the boys more extravagant. But I suppose I am a back number. I suppose I have got to come down with an additional subscription for the deficit. I am not always a cheerful giver.[1]

Brother Rice was so concerned about expenses getting out of hand that he attended the regular house meeting on May 11, 1921. He urged the undergraduates to "retrench" on expenses and specifically recommended that the junior reception be done away with.[2] The Society took his recommendation seriously and decided to cancel the reception for that year as well as to take other steps to reduce expenses. By the late spring of 1922, the financial crisis had moderated a bit, thanks to the subscription mentioned by Billy North Rice. Another piece of good financial news came in the form of a bequest from the estate of William P. Hubbard (1863) who had died the previous year. He left a sum of up to $10,000 for an endowment fund, which had to be matched by gifts from others in order to enter into effect. The endowment fund was formally established by a change to the Socratic Bylaws at the Annual Meeting of June 17, 1922. Matching funds were raised through subscription, and it was announced at the next Annual Meeting (June 15, 1923) that $21,350 had been added to the endowment as a result. Although continuing problems with the leaky roof and a leaky shower room with attendant damage to the dining room ceiling required expensive repairs, undergraduate attention to cost-cutting allowed an overall increase of $600 of income over expenses in the annual financial report presented at the Socrats' Annual Meeting of June 13, 1924.

From 1925 to the end of the decade the financial situation had its ups and downs. Extraordinary expenses resulting from a lightning strike on the house in the summer of 1925, and especially from the breakdown of the heating system in the winter of 1928–29 caused temporary negative cash flows, but the general financial condition of the house improved in the last half of the decade. Two factors appear to have accounted for much of the improved situation: an increased attention to stewardship of resources and timely payment of bills on the part of the undergraduates—and an increase in the number of members (i.e., dues-payers) initiated into the Society as the decade progressed. This increase in size caused misgivings on the part of some Socrats, as will be discussed later.

The second major theme that runs through the 1920s is concern with the academic standing of the Society and its members. The undergraduates themselves recognized the problem in the first meeting of the academic year 1919–20. Eclectic's standing in the Jackson Cup[3] competition for the previous year was described as a "catastrophe" (the House fell from first to second place). Brother Raymond A. Dousseau made a plea for better scholarship.[4] The plea went unheeded for a number of years, if one takes first place (of eleven) in the Jackson Cup competition as the primary measure of scholarship. Eclectic maintained its second place in 1920, but then began a descent from third place in 1921 to fourth place in 1922 and 1923. There was a rally in 1924 (third place) and again in 1925 (second place), but the Fraternity slipped to fourth place again in 1926 and vacillated between second and third for four successive years until a return to first place (and much rejoicing) in 1930.[5]

Throughout the period of less-than-stellar academic accomplishments, a number of appeals were made in house meetings for increased effort. The minutes of November 29, 1920, include the Scholarship Committee's report that marks were "exceedingly low" and its request for cooperation in raising them. Positive steps were reported in the minutes of January 5, 1922, when the House affirmed that the Scholarship Committee had full power to regulate and enforce freshman study hours. It became a requirement during this period that freshman had to maintain good marks in order to be initiated, and the record of initiations indicate that the rule was enforced (i.e., an increase in number of delayed initiations). There are repeated references to "low scholarship grades" (or similar phrases) in weekly meetings during these years, along with appeals for improvement.

While the undergraduates were concerned with Eclectic's academic standing, the Socrats were, in some cases, beside themselves. Billy North Rice was in the forefront of those urging academic excellence as a hallmark of Eclectic. In his report as chairman of the Board of Directors in 1920, he pointed out that nonfraternity men (e.g., the Commons Club) had taken over the lead in Jackson Cup competition. Eclectic, while not covering itself with dishonor, was not living up to its earlier record. Quoting figures from 1909 to 1919, he pointed out that of twenty-five high honors awarded at graduation, only five had been to Eclectics.[6] He opined that the elegance of the new House had a deleterious effect on scholarship. The next year, 1921, the academic section of his report focused on the freshman delegation. He laid the blame for their generally low scholastic achievement on the increasingly wide area from which students were recruited and the hurried nature of rushing. These two factors led to election of freshmen whose backgrounds were not really well known. His solution was to urge alumni to get to know members of the incoming class and to provide input to the cultivation process.[7] Brother Rice's concerns were not unfounded. The number of nongraduates in the delegations of 1921 through 1924 was significantly higher than in most previous years, a possible indicator of academic problems, but also a reflection of Wesleyan's declining graduation rate during this period.[8] From 1925 on, the number declined to normal levels, and even with the significantly larger delegations at the end of the decade, nongraduates did not represent a significant figure. Academically, the House was back on track.

The perceived increased emphasis on parties and social life during the 1920s was mainly a concern of the Socratic Literary Society and its Board of Directors, led by Billy North Rice. He, above all others, commented a number of times on the matter. His perspective was that the elegance of the house and the consequent increased number of social events led to a bad effect on scholarship and other traditional Eclectic virtues, including sobriety. He urged on several occasions that the number of dances per year be reduced, and the undergraduates responded positively. After all, they were dealing with the man described by many as "the greatest Eclectic." He addressed a few words to the Annual Meeting of the Society on June 15, 1928, but it was obvious that his health was failing. He died on November 14, 1928, a week shy of his eighty-third birthday.[9]

Among Brother Rice's concerns in the early 1920s were the cost, size, and composition of the Fraternity. The rise in costs to undergraduates (e.g., term tax of $22 for house residents and $21 for others in 1919[10] to $46 for house residents and $44 for others in 1921)[11] led him to warn in the June 13, 1924, Board of Directors report to the Socrats' Annual Meeting that the poor might be excluded from membership—an adverse consequence, to his mind. He expressed another concern in referring to the size of the delegation of 1928. Although that delegation was possessed of above-average scholarship, its number of eighteen (later twenty) was nearly double that of previous delegations. He worried that such large delegations would lead to undesirable consequences for the Society. He opined that the whole Society should not number more than forty (i.e., about ten per delegation). Another problem that he addressed was that of the selection of "born men." If strictly observed, it drove the number in delegations up.[12] He voiced the same concern of "hereditary right" to membership and its relation to the size of the Fraternity at the Socrats' Annual Meeting the next year.[13]

Although the four issues discussed to this point in the chapter were serious, they pale before the major problem of the decade: the consumption of alcohol, both in and outside the House. The minutes of both Phi Nu Theta and the Socratic Literary Society and its Board of Directors are replete with references to the problem. Of course, it was the era of Prohibition, and the manufacture, sale, or transportation of intoxicating liquors was forbidden by the Eighteenth Amendment to the U.S. Constitution, which went into effect at the beginning of 1920 and remained so until repealed at the end of 1933. Although consumption of intoxicating beverages was not prohibited per se, their acquisition implied a violation of federal law. There was a particularly offensive series of incidents at the 1920 Thanksgiving dance at the House, and the behavior was formally deplored at the next house meeting.[14] Further action was taken in March when the brothers approved the following motion: "In the future, the possession of liquor in any form, externally or internally, by any member of the House shall automatically place him on censure."[15] A week later, further penalties were attached to the consumption (and later possession) of alcoholic beverages on the property, beginning with censure and suspension from the Alpha Club for a week for a first offense, to absolute and indefinite suspension from the Fraternity for a third offense.[16] The new rule was enforced. Fifteen brothers suffered the punishment for a first violation (censure and suspension from the Alpha Club) at the beginning of April 1921.[17]

The Socrats were very concerned and called for the creation of a liquor committee in the House. The undergraduates concurred and voted to form one—to be constituted after the next dance.[18] Still, the problem of drinking in the House and general disregard for the law of the land occupied a significant portion of the Socrats' Annual Meeting on June 17, 1921. The tension between at least some undergraduates and their elders is evident in the minutes of that meeting. Billy North Rice took early action to try to avoid a repetition of the events of 1920–21 when he addressed the first regular fraternity meeting of 1921–22. He reminded the brothers of rules governing dancing and drinking in brotherly but firm terms.[19]

Violations of the no-drinking rule occurred over the next few years, but the violators were increasingly recent graduates rather than under-graduates. The minutes of March 12, 1924, report that a letter was sent from the Society to its younger alumni asking them not to bring liquor into the House. The undergraduates also asked the Socrats for assis-tance in the matter.[20] By 1925, almost all reported violations of the liquor rule were by returning alumni rather than by undergraduates, and the incidence declined rapidly. By vote of the House, the liquor rule was read aloud at the first meeting after each initiation.[21] The education program, a reform spirit in the House, and pressure from the Socrats produced results. No violations were reported in 1928,[22] and mention of the problem essentially disappears from the records thereafter.

Two responses to the call for information issued in conjunction with the effort to develop a history of the Fraternity for the 1937 Centen-nial celebration give immediate personal perspectives on the decade. Edward M. Thorndike (1926), member of a distinguished Eclectic fam-ily, wrote of his years (1922–26):

Alpha Club: Freshmen were initiated into the Alpha Club each fall. Although the seriousness of the fraternity initiation was lacking, the ceremony was impressive. . . . Just before Christmas vacation, the club held a Christmas dinner. It was an elaborate affair, com-pared with our usual meals, at which presents of a humorous nature were given to a selected group of members.

During the time Brother Stephen Henry Olin was acting Presi-dent of the University, Mrs. Olin took a keen interest in the Fra-ternity. She had the large oil paintings restored, gave rugs and many other things to improve the appearance of the House. . . . [To thank her, a plan was adopted] to make her an honorary mem-ber of the Alpha Club. An elaborate certificate was prepared. The Olins were asked to dinner and Brother Jack Dunn (1923) made the presentation in a most impressive manner. It was a great success.

During this period, it was customary for a senior to be seated at the head and a freshman at the foot of each of seven or eight tables. The former served meats, etc., and the latter butter and water. Seniors filled the office of "President of the Dining Hall"

["Proedros" in the Weekly Meeting context] by rotation each week . . . and during their incumbency called upon various brothers for grace before meals and endeavored to maintain general dining hall decorum. In the latter duty, the "President" was assisted by a self-appointed "gutter gang" comprising about six of the huskier brothers, who upon infraction of an Alpha Club rule would seize the offender and deposit him unceremoniously in the High Street gutter.

Frolics and Customs: At some time during the winter, it was customary for the freshman delegation to entertain the other members with the "Freshman Charades." These consisted of a number of skits written and enacted by members of the freshman delegation in which an attempt was made to ridicule the members of the Society, particularly the seniors and the faculty. I believe the custom died in 1925 or 1926.

Sunday evening sings in the library were held more or less regularly during this period. Often members of the faculty were invited to dinner and the sings. Most of the brothers enjoyed the sings and often a group would form around the piano afterwards and continue in an informal way. An inter-fraternity singing contest was held, I believe, in 1925 in which the Fraternity placed second.

Three dances were held by the Fraternity each year, one in the fall, one in the winter after midyear examinations, and one in the spring. In general, there was dancing on Friday and Saturday evenings. Almost all of the undergraduate members of the Fraternity attended and enjoyed these parties, at which there was little formality, partners being selected by the "cut-in" method.

The game of "konk," closely resembling shuffleboard, played on the rectangular living room table with half dollars, became so popular at one time that it appeared to be having an injurious effect on the Society's scholastic standing and was therefore restricted by House action to certain hours. Other forms of indoor amusement were "double solitaire" played by eight or ten brothers around a large circular table, and Ping-Pong.

The Atmosphere of the Society. It is impossible for me to characterize the main interests of the Society group because the individual members had quite different interests and ideals. It may be said, however, that the Fraternity was represented by outstanding men in practically all phases of college life, both scholastic and extra-curricular.

The Society and Other Wesleyan Fraternities: The relations between Eclectic and other fraternities were cordial. There were no particular favorites. We had friends in all.

The Socratic Literary Society: I would like to note here that the relations between the undergraduates and the resident directors became much more friendly during my four years. Relations had been rather strained, but a fine spirit of cooperation existed during the years 1925–26. Brother [William George] Chanter [(1914)] deserves the highest praise, for it was he, I think, who was largely responsible for this.[23]

Howard B. Matthews (1928), later vice president and treasurer of Wesleyan, also submitted a response to the plea for input to the planned history. His recollections covered the period 1924–28 and parallel those of Brother Thorndike in many respects but offer a different perspective on some topics:

The Alpha Club. Meals "fit for a king" were served at Thanksgiving, Christmas, Washington's Birthday, Easter, Halloween, etc. with appropriate table decorations. Miss Farnsworth [the Matron] took great pride in the latter and spent weeks preparing them; [she] never felt that "the boys" quite appreciated her efforts. Meals throughout the year were uniformly good, but elicited the usual complaints.

A variation [of the gutter gang's depositing an offender in the High Street gutter] was to deposit the yearling, naked, on the library hearth, where he was purged with a few shovels of cold wood ash.

The custom of singing college and fraternity songs after meals was continued and improved throughout the period, particularly under the leadership of [H. Calvin] Kuhl (1927).

Eclectic Frolics and Customs. [Concerning the spring, winter, and fall dances,] strictly adhered to was the custom of delegating to a committee the duty of a formal call on Billy Rice and Morry Crawford to ask their approval of the use of the House for a dance. They never refused.

There was the usual "riding" of freshmen prior to initiation, although this never amounted to hazing. It usually consisted of requiring the newcomers to sing their prep school songs, recite or sing Eclectic and college songs, the names (in full) of the brothers. These exercises were confined to the hour following dinner, after which the freshmen were ordered to their rooms for study. There was none of the time-wasting foolery such as was carried on by other houses.

The Atmosphere of the Society. The interests of the Society during this period embraced both curricular and extra-curricular. There was apparent a decided turning from the carefree attitude of the immediately preceding delegations to the more serious-minded attitude, which has ever since been more and more a characteristic of Eclectics. I do not mean that interests were narrowed; rather, there was exhibited an attempt to participate in all of the college activities and at the same time to bring Eclectic back to the top scholastically. . . .

The Society and Other Wesleyan Fraternities. The relationship. . . . was cordial. A round-robin system whereby senior delegations of other fraternities were entertained at dinner by Eclectic was in effect during this period. Eclectic's studious and serious attitude, while sometimes mistaken for snobbishness, was respected.[24]

In Brother Matthews's paragraph on the "riding of freshmen" he mentions the requirement that they learn fraternity songs, the full names of brothers, and so on. In the 1950s, the custom continued and was called a "line up." With the exception of "the Charter Gag," to be discussed later, it was as close to hazing as Eclectic came, but neither was really hazing, for both served a real purpose and did not threaten physical harm. Although not mentioned in Brother Matthews's piece, the requirement that each freshman pledge carry a black book, where a record of infringements could be recorded, was observed as early as 1920. An item in the minutes of that year record that only sophomores could make entries in the pledges' black books.[25]

A few additional themes that ran through the 1920s need to be mentioned in closing this chapter. Dress at dinner and meetings was always a topic of discussion. After wavering between formality and informality, the brothers opted for the more formal stiff collar (i.e., tie) and jacket at least at meetings and the dinners that preceded them. The House fielded an amazing number of teams for interfraternity competition. At one time or another there were teams in track, football, basketball, baseball, tennis, swimming, handball, and bowling. Much of the impetus came from Dr. Edgar Fauver, college physician and professor of physical education, who strongly supported an interfraternity sports competition program. Evidently the pressure of fielding all these teams got to the brothers; they approved a resolution at the weekly meeting of January 9, 1925, urging that interfraternity sports be limited to baseball, basketball, and tennis. It appears to have had no effect. Literary exercises followed the traditional pattern of two analyses of essays, two essays, two criticisms, and one or two special oral topics. The term "essay" was used in the most general sense, for short stories, plays, and occasional original poems appeared more and more frequently in the bulletin of literary exercises.

The Society lost a number of illustrious alumni during the decade, most prominently, William P. Hubbard (1863) in 1921 and William North Rice (1865) in 1928, but also James A. Develin (1883) in 1923 and Stephen Henry Olin (1866) in 1925. Most Eclectics of later years knew Brother Olin as the author of the fraternity song "Tela Mystica," the fraternity equivalent of an alma mater, sung with great emotion at every annual meeting, initiation, and formal ceremony where undergraduates and graduates assembled. Older alumni knew him as a generous donor to the House, as acting president of the University during the illness of President Shanklin (1922–23), and as son of Wesleyan's third president, Stephen Olin. The Olin Memorial Library was named in memory of father and son, and both were laid to rest in the little cemetery on Foss Hill.

Eclectic was still being courted by other fraternities in the 1920s. The minutes of February 22, 1922, report a motion of sentiment against affiliation with Phi Delta Sigma. The same year witnessed the establishment of the Founders' Prize. The prize was to be awarded at each Annual Meeting to two members of either the junior or sophomore classes who according to active members (i.e., undergraduates) "most faithfully and effectively encouraged others in the maintenance of Eclectic traditions and ideals of character."[26] The prize was established by Nelson C. Hubbard (1892), son of the recently deceased William P. Hubbard (1863) and grandson of Chester D. Hubbard (1840). Brother Nelson Hubbard presented the first prizes to John A. Dunn (1923) and Edward G. Budd (1923) at the 1922 Annual Meeting.[27]

Occasionally, well-known persons from the world of politics, literature, or the arts visited the House. The minutes of November 13, 1922, indicate that Professor C. Wilbert Snow, Professor of English for many years, invited renowned American poet Carl Sandburg to read at a meeting of friends held at Eclectic. Less famous but equally welcome guests occupied the House on dance weekends in the latter part of the decade. Minutes of Weekly Meetings on February 2, 1926, and November 8, 1929, indicate that it was the custom on at least some dance weekends for the resident brothers to seek accommodations elsewhere and turn the House over to the female guests. There was an indication that Billy North Rice was not in favor of the arrangement in 1926, but he did not insist.

This same time frame saw a debate concerning seating in Eclectic Hall during Weekly Meetings. Minutes of the Annual Meeting of June 18, 1926, report that there was a sentiment for "no more segregation by classes" in meetings, so that the democratic spirit of the House would be reflected. At an early meeting of the year 1926–27 a compromise was reached: the senior delegation would sit against the east wall of the room, while all others would "intermingle."[28] Since this was before the initiation of any freshmen in the Delegation of 1930, it is not clear whether they would be included in the intermingling. In the 1950s, seniors continued to sit along the east wall of Eclectic Hall, the juniors and sophomores sat with no distinction as to delegation along the south wall, and freshmen sat as a delegation along the north wall. I rather suspect that the arrangement, established in the fall of 1926, was the one we observed thirty years later.

The *Scroll*, the fraternity newspaper to inform alumni of undergraduate activities, began publication in the fall of 1926.[29] Over the years it appeared at various intervals, but most often twice a year, and it was still being published in the 1950s. The publication of the *Scroll* can be taken as a sign of the improving relations between the under-graduates and their older brothers in the Socratic Literary Society. By the end of the decade, relations were back to their old cordiality, some-thing that had been badly affected by low scholastic achievement and violation of the no-drinking policy in the early part of the decade. The Board of Directors report to the last Socrats Annual Meeting of the de-cade, delivered by Professor Morris B. Crawford (1874), is full of praise for the undergraduates. Even finances were on a fairly even keel, de-spite the "slump," the first reference to the Great Depression to appear in the records.[30] Its effects, however, were to be keenly felt as the de-pression deepened in the 1930s.

he decade was one of more consistent and remarkably successful attention to the Society's scholastic status, as reflected in the Jackson Cup competition. For the first time in twelve years, Eclectic placed first in 1930, and then, after two years of falling to second and third place, regained first place for three successive years (1933, 1934, and 1935), thereby retaining possession of the cup. Moreover, Eclectic won the Cup again in 1936, 1937, and 1938, making six successive wins. The undergraduates were extremely proud of their record, and the Socrats were ecstatic, especially Professor Morris B. Crawford (1874) and Professor Burton H. Camp (1901), whose stint as chairman of the Board of Directors started in 1932–33. There was not universal joy, however, at the scholastic triumph of Phi Nu Theta. According to Kenneth R. Andrews (1936) in an interview with David Potts on July 2, 2002, Wesleyan President McConaughy "lectured" him during the course of a meeting in the presidential office on Eclectic's strategy of targeting Olin scholars during fall rushes. In rather "stern" words McConaughy opined to Brother Andrews that this was a too one-dimensional approach to selecting members and also a strategy potentially harmful to the healthy distribution of top students among all fraternities.[1]

At the Socrats' Annual Meeting of June 17, 1930, a rather strange incident occurred in view of subsequent events. The college Class of 1890 asked permission to install a marker on the front lawn at 200 High Street to commemorate the fact that Woodrow Wilson, twenty-eighth president of the United States, lived in a house on that spot while he was a professor at Wesleyan (1888–90). The motion to permit the installation of the marker was "lost" (i.e., not approved). Such a marker, a brass plaque on a stone, was eventually installed, for it was certainly there in the late 1950s.[2] It disappeared at some point after that time.

The year 1931 involved much activity associated with the celebration of the Centennial of Wesleyan, which took place October 10–12 of that year. Many Eclectics, both Socrats and undergraduates, contributed to planning and carrying out the festivities. Chief among these were Professor Karl S. Van Dyke (1916), who served as executive secretary of committee, and the Hon. Frederick M. Davenport, Member of Congress (1889), who delivered the principal address at the formal ceremony. In the House, a new *Songs of Phi Nu Theta* was published in honor of the Centennial.[3] It was to serve as the definitive song book for the duration of the existence of the Fraternity in its traditional form.[4] Carl Price wrote his *Wesleyan's First Century* (published in 1932), which evidently stirred thoughts of a similar effort to mark the Centennial of the Fraternity six years in the future. A graduating senior, John A. Kouwenhoven (1931), later an author of books on American history, first raised the subject at the June 12, 1931, Annual Meeting of the Socrats. During a fraternity meeting held in conjunction with the University's Centennial weekend, October 10–12, 1931, Eric M. North (1909) presented a tentative outline of the proposed history of Eclectic. The undergraduates recommended to the Socrats that they authorize up to $200 for "stenographic help."[5]

During the course of 1931–32, William W. Martin (1874) offered a bequest to the Socratic Literary Society to establish a Martin Prize, which was accepted by the Annual Meeting of the Socrats of June 17, 1932. The prize, consisting of the interest income from the bequest of $1000, was to be awarded annually to the freshman with the highest record of achievement at midyear. The recipient each year would be obligated to read several historical documents relating to the Fraternity, including an address of the donor. According to the terms of the bequest, the corpus would revert with no restrictions to the general funds of the Socratic Literary Society twenty-one years after the death of the last member of the Delegations of 1928 through 1932. The first prize was presented by Professor Crawford, a delegation mate of the donor, to cowinners Clarence K. Aldrich and Horace K. Burr of the Delegation of 1935 at the regular fraternity meeting held on March 9, 1932. A listing of all recorded Martin Prize recipients is included in appendix C.

Indications of a changing attitude toward the consumption of alcoholic beverages began to appear early in the decade. There is no record of a reading of the liquor rule following the regular initiation (fifteen freshmen) of November 7, 1931. Then in May 1932, the undergradu-

ates formally expressed a sentiment of the House against the "strin-
gent application" of the liquor rule.[6] There is no reaction in Socratic
Literary Society minutes to the undergraduates' "sentiment" for four
years. In 1936, however, Brother Burton H. Camp in his report as chair
of the Board of Directors noted that Prohibition was over and that, although formal Socrat policy remained against drinking in the House
in general, the undergraduates had modified their approach to punish
"intemperance" rather than possession or consumption. (A new liquor
rule to this effect was formally incorporated into the bylaws at the regular May 13, 1936, fraternity meeting.) In Brother Camp's opinion, the
arrangement was working and drunkenness was not a major problem
at Phi Nu Theta.[7]

Prior to 1932 there are surprisingly few references to the Great Depression that so marked the generation that grew up in the years between the "crash" of October 1929 and the entry of the United States
into World War II in December 1941. The effects on the Fraternity were
certainly of concern, however, by the time of the Annual Socratic Literary Society Meeting of June 17, 1932. The minutes discuss the threat of
an exodus of students because of financial difficulties. Actions taken
to try to ameliorate the situation had included a general cutting of expenses and most especially those associated with the cost of food and
the number of dances. The following year, a reference to the effect of
the economic situation resulting in lower contributions by Socrats appeared in the minutes, along with more specifics of cost-cutting efforts.
Eclectic annual dues were reduced from $102 in 1931–32 to $74.50 in
1932–33. Dances were limited to two, and they were voluntary. Alpha
Club boarding rates were held to $8 per week in comparison to other
fraternities, which charged $8.50 for their dining clubs.[8] Despite these
efforts, a brother, Herbert R. Houghton (1935), was forced to withdraw
from the fraternity for financial reasons. The Society absolved him of
fraternal obligations and voted to consider him an alumnus.[9] He graduated with his class in June 1935.

The worst effects of the Great Depression on Eclectic and its members appear to have disappeared by the beginning of 1934–35. The last
specific mention of them was at the Socrats' Annual Meeting of June 15,
1934. The minutes of that meeting address the continued lower rate
of alumni contributions to the Socratic Literary Society and a nagging

problem of late payment of bills by undergraduate Eclectics; the blame is laid at the door of the Great Depression. Two brothers were exempted from paying dues as late as 1936–37, but in general, allusions to the economic crisis disappear from the records in the mid-1930s.

Weekly literary exercises at meetings remained central to the Fraternity. A perusal of literary appointments as set forth in the minutes shows that religion was far less often a topic of essays than in previous decades. Creative writing in the form of short stories, occasional poetry, and even an original play became much more frequent, a fact noted with some concern in Professor Crawford's last report as chairman of the board at the 1932 Annual Meeting of the Socrats.[10] The high quality of literary exercises, however, was noted in Professor Camp's first report as chairman of the Board of Directors to the Socrats' Annual Meeting the next year, although unexcused comings and goings at weekly meetings had a negative effect on proceedings.[11] Surprisingly, few essays addressed the world economic and political situation. An exception came in the form of two essays presented to the Hall on the same evening in the fall of 1933: "Ein Turnfest für Hitler" ("A Gymnastic Display for Hitler") and "Possibilities of War in Europe."[12] Later in the decade, more references to the world situation appear with such topics as "Is America Prepared for War?" and "Caricatures of Adolph Hitler" on the list of appointments for the spring of 1938.[13]

The format of literary exercised was modified slightly in the spring of 1936; once a month, a debate replaced special topics and only one written essay was presented.[14] The first debate recorded in the minutes after the change was probably a lively one. The topic was "Resolved that persons should be allowed to participate without social stigma in sexual intercourse during engagement." Interestingly, the decision was for the negative.[15] Seven months later, a debate took place on the topic "Resolved that Wesleyan should turn co-ed." The minutes do not reflect what decision on the debate was reached, but the discussion was lively.[16]

Another hot topic was addressed in literary exercises toward the end of the decade. Two special topics were included in the exercises as reported in the minutes for April 12, 1938. The first was a prepared oral presentation, "Maraisana, the Assassin of Youth," and the second, extemporaneous: "My Experience with Maraisana." If one substitutes the contemporary spelling of the word, "marijuana," the import of the presentations becomes clear. I doubt we would have addressed the topic in the same way in the late 1950s.

The matron system of adult supervision of the day-to-day running of the House lasted until the end of the decade. From the earliest days of the Society's owning its own facility, retaining matrons and/or cooks had been a recurring problem. Although specific references in both Eclectic and Socrat records are scarce, at least six different matrons were hired between 1902 and 1938.[17] The last of these, a Mrs. West, apparently provoked some unhappiness. Brothers were cautioned at the Regular Meeting of May 30, 1934, not to use her telephone. The prohibition must have had some unpleasant history, because later at the same meeting a motion was made to urge the Socrats that Mrs. West be let go. The motion evidently did not carry, and no mention of the sentiment appears in the Socrat minutes for that year. In the fall of the year, Board of Directors chairman Professor Burton Camp attended a regular House Meeting and addressed the matron matter. The sentiment of the House had changed since May. A vote indicated that the brothers now favored the matron system, with Mrs. West as matron.[18] This positive sentiment was reaffirmed by vote of the House toward the end of the academic year.[19]

Two years later matters had changed again. At a meeting in the fall of 1937, the House went on record as not favoring the matron system.[20] Mrs. West is described as the "former housekeeper" in the Socrats' Annual Meeting minutes of June 17, 1938, but they noted that she had a concession to furnish meals until June 15. The minutes also mention that the Alpha Club had ceased to exist as a separate entity. It was now formally a part of the Fraternity (although nonfraternity members could still board in it). Lastly, it was announced at the June 1938 Socrat Meeting that Erich Fichtner and his wife would take over the dining concession in the fall of 1938 and would live in the House. Also employed would be a houseman (a Mr. Mulvaney),[21] technically the only employee of the Fraternity, since the Fichtners were concessionaires. For those who remember with fondness "The Chief," Erich Fichtner, and his wife Kaethe, 1938–39 marked the beginning of a remarkable relationship that endured for more than twenty years.

The year 1937 marked the one hundredth anniversary of the Eclectic Society of Phi Nu Theta. Preliminary planning for a suitable celebration of the event had begun as early as 1931, when the Centennial of the University reminded both undergraduates and graduates that only six years would separate the two events. Specific plans were laid at a Special Meeting of the Socratic Literary Society following the initiation of the Delegation of 1940 on November 13, 1936. The meeting, attended by ninety (including undergraduates), settled on the Friday, November 5, 1937, for private exercises and Saturday, November 6, 1937, for the public celebration. The following was proposed: (1) a sub-rosa supper, initiation, regular Society meeting with special literary exercises to include the reading of essays written for meetings in the 1860s by Billy North Rice and Stephen Henry Olin with criticisms by undergraduates in the Society in 1937 and (2) public exercises in the '92 Theater the following day, the program to be determined. In preparation for the Centennial, the House was to be renovated, and the undergraduates were asked to submit a list of the most pressing needs.[22] The undergraduates responded in June 1937 with a number of recommendations, primarily new living room furniture, as well as refurbishment of rooms and studies.[23]

The actual Centennial Celebrations were conducted more or less as planned on the agreed dates with the addition of a grand Centennial Banquet in the House following the initiation meeting on Friday.[24] The public exercises on Saturday, November 6, in the '92 Theater consisted of a brief welcome by Henry Ingraham Harriman (1895), who chaired the proceedings; an address by Wesleyan President McConaughy; the singing of "Phi Nu Theta Floreat" by an Eclectic sextet; a Centennial Address by Congressman Frederick M. Davenport (1889); the singing of "With Joyful Songs We Come" by the sextet; the unveiling of a portrait of Billy North Rice (1865) conducted by his son Edward L. Rice (1892); and, as a concluding rite, the singing by all of "Tela Mystica" (referred to in the program as "The Fraternity Hymn"). By all accounts, the whole celebration on both days was most impressive.

The Centennial provided an opportunity to strengthen positive feelings toward the Fraternity. There were indications that antifraternity sentiments were beginning to arise on the campus in middecade among some members of the faculty and administration. The proposal by a faculty-student committee in 1933–34 that freshmen be required to eat in their own dining room, part of the "College Union Plan," was greeted with great concern by the Socrats in the person of Professor Camp. He foresaw that it would entail deferred rushing and elimination of initiation of freshmen. As chairman of the Board of Directors, he undertook to discuss the matter with President McConaughy, urging careful deliberation of any such scheme.[25] His efforts appear to have contributed to a deferral of further action on the proposal, although the subject resurfaced in the late 1950s with the construction of new freshman dorms. The antifraternity attitude of "many" members of the faculty and administration was brought up again the following year in Professor Camp's report.[26] In it he observed that Alpha Delta Phi and Psi Upsilon were known to have literary exercises, and they, along with Eclectic, were the strongest fraternities. He suggested that other fraternities be urged to emulate the leading ones in order to present a strong and serious answer to those who challenged the right to existence of such organizations.

A number of miscellaneous points about the decade of the Great Depression should be noted. Attendance at meetings was sometimes less than perfect and undergraduates, encouraged by resident Socrats, took a number of steps to ensure that members observed the requirement to attend all meetings unless formally excused. Dress continued to be a matter of debate. As in the previous decade, guidance for more formal attire (e.g., respectable dark clothes and no sports shoes) at dinner and weekly meetings alternated with permission for more casual wear (e.g., white shoes were permissible at dinner and meetings in May and June one year).

Finger-snapping continued to be a campus tradition but was modified by decision of the College Senate in 1930. Henceforth, the custom was not to be observed in chapel.[27] The brothers were urged to support the decision by their actions. Dances during the Great Depression were sometimes cosponsored with other fraternities to save expenses. Alpha Delta Phi and Psi Upsilon were on several occasions cosponsors of such events. During the height of the depression, dance taxes were strictly voluntary. By 1933–34, however, dances were again compulsory (and therefore taxable) events.

There was some concern expressed in 1936 and 1937 that a rift might be developing again between the Socrats and the undergraduate Fraternity. The Socrats adopted two measures at the urging of Professor Camp to ameliorate the situation by increasing formal contact between the two. First, occasional meetings of the Socratic Literary Society would be held at the time of initiation (as was the case in 1936), and second, two seniors would henceforth sit on the Board of Directors of the Socrats.[28] Talk of a rift disappeared from the minutes thereafter.

Death claimed two prominent Socrats during the decade. Ashley H. Thorndike (1893), distinguished professor of English at Columbia University, died in 1933, and Frank Mason North (1872), renowned Methodist clergyman, in 1935. Both were Wesleyan Trustees (North for thirty-six years) and members of multigenerational Eclectic families. Brothers "draped their keys" out of respect for the illustrious departed. The last occasion for this ritual had been at the death of Billy North Rice in 1928.

Eclectic had weathered the Great Depression of the 1930s and gone from strength to strength in many areas, particularly scholarship. War clouds were gathering in the last part of the decade and war, of course, broke out in Europe in September 1939. An item in the minutes of the Socrats' Annual Meeting of June 16, 1939, foreshadowed things to come. German and English foreign students in the Alpha Club "fought out wars over teacups and not with weapons under the cook's watchful eye." The Chief, Erich Fichtner, was born in Germany, and the coming struggle would put enormous emotional strains on him and his wife. America's entry into World War II two years later was to affect every aspect of American life. Wesleyan and Eclectic did not escape the consequences.

nnual fraternity dues for 1939–40 were raised from $96 to $100.[1] Although the effects of the Great Depression had faded, they had not disappeared completely. A brother was voted into inactive status, evidently at his own request, because of financial pressures. At a subsequent meeting, the Society voted to assume the cost of the dues of the financially embarrassed senior. More and more the Alpha Club (eating club) came to be viewed as a source of potential members. The minutes of December 6, 1939, reflect a change in rules so that a two-thirds vote was required for election to the Alpha Club. Pledging was an explicit goal for persons so elected. In the spring of 1940, by vote of the House, the Alpha Club was closed to members of other fraternities whose own eating clubs were closed, further reinforcing the cultivation nature of the eating club, at least for a while.[2]

The rules governing initiation were also modified. An average of at least seventy-three was required for any marking period for a pledge to be initiated.[3] Scholarship continued very definitely a consideration in selection of potential members. A further constraint on pledges' initiation is reflected in the minutes of May 1, 1940. A procedure was established whereby a secret ballot would be taken on all freshmen pledges as a group prior to fall initiation. If there was any dissenting vote, individual secret ballots would be taken on the prospective initiates. As the year 1939–40 drew to a close, the Annual Meeting of the Eclectic Society of Phi Nu Theta held on June 14 was particularly well attended; 110 were present, of whom 30 were undergraduates. William G. Chanter (1914)—in the absence in hospital of Morris B. Crawford (1874)—presented the Founders Prize to Brothers Hussong and Moore (both 1941). The same number of graduates and undergraduates stayed to attend the Annual Meeting of the Socratic Literary Society. With the advent of war, attendance at both Annual Meetings would drop sharply.

War clouds were still a distance away as 1940–41 got under way. Normal business proceeded: brass room plaques, recording the residents of each room in the House, were updated; freshman rules for "Hell Week" were spelled out; the sophomores were charged with recovering the stolen Jackson Cup and other miscellaneous items from the Psi Upsilon "Goat Room." Professor Crawford, the unofficial "grand old man" of Eclectic since the death of Billy Rice twelve years before, died at eighty-eight on October 9, 1940. His passing was noted in a resolution of the Regular Meeting of November 6, 1940, directing the placement of a memorial plate on the gavel used by the Proedros (presiding senior) at meetings.

The war in Europe and the general political climate are reflected in literary exercises of the period. Many essays for the Hall have to do with Nazism, the penetration of the ideology into the Americas, Hitler, and even "The Case for National Socialism." There are a few references to Japan, especially in connection with its war against China. On a more personal level, Alpha Club rules were relaxed in April 1941 to admit "refugee students"[4] to the dining hall. The war was drawing closer.

The Annual Meetings of the Fraternity and the Socratic Literary Society for 1941 were held sequentially (as had become the custom) on June 13. Besides the awarding of the Founders Prize by William G. Chanter (1914), who appears to have replaced the late Professor Crawford as the Grand Old Man of Eclectic, the fraternity minutes reveal that Psi Upsilon was still in possession of Eclectic memorabilia, including the retired Jackson Cup. The sophomores having failed to regain possession, Brother Chanter, as a revered alumnus, was asked to negotiate their return with his counterparts in Psi U. Attendance was down considerably from the previous year at the SLS Annual Meeting. Only thirty-eight Socrats and twenty undergraduates attended. The sum of $1,000 was earmarked to finance the completion of the history of Eclectic that had been intended for publication at the time of the Centennial in 1937. A committee was appointed to look into the revived proposal to place a plaque on the front lawn to commemorate the fact that Woodrow Wilson lived in a house on the site during his tenure at Wesleyan. A memorabilia committee, successor to a key committee, was chartered to look to the storage and preservation of Eclectic memorabilia. Two years before, the key committee's responsibility had been set as collecting for preservation the keys of deceased brothers.[5] Interestingly, the Socrats at the Annual Meeting made a distinction that was not necessarily observed either previously or subsequently: the term "The Eclectic Fraternity"—or "The Fraternity"—was reserved for the undergraduate organization, while "The Socratic Literary Society"—or "The Society" was restricted to the alumni organization. Finally, besides memorializing the death of Professor Crawford, the Socrats authorized the placement of a plaque in the chapel in memory of William North Rice (1865). The plaque was placed in a formal ceremony on November 9, 1941.[6]

Early in 1941–42, the nature of the Alpha Club changed again. Previously, new members had gone through an initiation ceremony. The custom was abolished by vote of the Regular Meeting of October 15, 1941. Although the Alpha Club served as a cultivating ground for prospective new members into the 1960s, it also served as a place where congenial undergraduates who would not or could not join the Fraternity forged friendships with members. Both social and financial forces drove this change—as well as a later campuswide program of having foreign students eat as guests of fraternity eating clubs. With the coming of war on December 7, 1941, however, everything changed again, and in most radical ways.

All restrictions on Alpha Club membership were suspended "for the duration" in early February 1942.[7] Fraternity eating clubs were closing, and Eclectic helped take up the slack for a while. On a University level, the second semester was shortened and commencement advanced to May 17. The first Wesleyan casualty of World War II was an Eclectic, Aviation Cadet Arthur Wilson Clothier (1941), killed on February 21, 1942.[8] Fifteen more Eclectics were to die as casualties of war before hostilities ended. Joint summer sessions with Trinity began on May 18, 1942, with six weeks at Wesleyan, six at Trinity. With the establishment of the U.S. Navy Flight Preparatory School (V-5) in January 1943, the reality of extraordinary wartime measures came home to Brothers in Eclectic. The Navy flier cadets took over dormitory rooms in Harriman and Clark Halls, and Eclectic freshmen who had lived there were obliged to move to a makeshift dormitory set up in the Goat Room.[9] Brother Mark Barlow (1946) commented, "I can't for the life of me recall where we held House meetings during the spring semester."[10] Brother Barlow further remembered that some of the older members, particularly juniors, who had already signed up with the Army Special Training

Program (ASTP) were prematurely called up in January 1943 and therefore left school. The eating club shrank despite members joining from other fraternities that had closed their eating clubs.

Erich and Kaethe Fichtner were a significant presence in the fraternity in these trying days. The war was particularly hard on them, too, as they were German immigrants and had close friends or relatives in the service on both sides. In fact, the deaths in quick succession of three or four brothers of the classes of 1940 and 1941, who were very close to Kaethe, almost certainly contributed to a complete nervous breakdown she suffered on the spring of 1943. Gone was her fastidious attention to cleanliness and order in the dining room, as well as the "open houses" she and the Chief used to hold in the parlor off the dining room. The Chief had to carry on alone until the decision was made to close the dining room and suspend Alpha Club operations in view of continually falling numbers and in conjunction with the Chief's accepting a position as assistant manager of the Pratt and Whitney plant cafeteria in Hartford. The plant was near the facility where Kaethe was undergoing treatment. True to his sense of duty to the House, the Chief prepared one final banquet before departing for his new position in a firm closely associated with the war effort.[11] He left with the express wish of undergraduates and Socrats that he and Kaethe return after the war.

During all this period, regular House meetings and literary exercises continued. Not surprisingly, many essays and special topics addressed war-related issues: salvage operations, avoiding inflation, the Japanese Air Force, big business and national defense, and so on. Attendance at meetings was described as "poor" by one frustrated Epistoleus.[12] Other signs abound that the wartime environment was not conducive to "business as usual." Records of initiation were not kept as meticulously as before and after the years 1943–45. Periods went by with no minutes of meetings copied into official records. For the first time ever, literary exercises were reduced to one analysis, one essay, one related criticism, and one special topic.[13] On a lighter note, neither the sophomores nor Brother Chanter had met any success in retrieving the missing memorabilia from Psi U. The Annual Meeting of May 16, 1942, deputized Brother Ralph F. Bischoff (1927), professor of government and treasurer of the SLS, as a committee of one to succeed in the venture.

The minutes of March 10, 1943, mention that acting president of the University Butterfield was to visit the House as a guest "in the near future." There is no confirmation that the visit actually occurred. It may have been put off as a result of the April 12, 1943, resignation of President McConaughy after eighteen years in the post and the eventual succession of "Vic" Butterfield to that office. Vic, who lived next door (brick house), had a cordial relationship with the House.[14] More on that anon.

At about the same time, there was discussion of turning the House into an officers' club,[15] but nothing came of it. More and more it appeared that the House might have to close down completely because of the paucity of undergraduates to carry on regular activities. As mentioned earlier, the eating club did cease functioning at the end of the term. Ralph Bischoff, treasurer of the Socrats, addressed the undergraduates at their Regular Meeting on April 14, 1943. Options and costs facing the Fraternity and Society included: the House shut tight ($2,300/year); shut, but heated and minor matters attended to ($3,300/year); only social rooms open (no estimate); kept open completely (regular costs); be made into a boardinghouse (no estimate).

The Annual Meetings of both organizations were held on May 29, 1943, with all undergraduates (twenty-two) not serving in the military in attendance. At the undergraduate meeting it was announced that rushing would be held the third week in July, a reflection of the fact that the college was now in session practically year-round for the duration —with three terms (summer, winter, and spring) and three associated commencements. At the alumni meeting it was announced that Mark Barlow (1946), with the help of Edward L. Rice (1892) and Paul North Rice (1910), had acquired the Minute Book of the Beta Chapter at Ohio Wesleyan University for retention in the archives.[16] The Socrats decided to keep the House open and used as much as possible until November 1, 1943, at which point the local Directors were empowered to take whatever decisions were necessary. The meetings concluded on a high note with pledges by Eclectics and Socrats to keep the flame alive. Specific measures included Socrat committees to manage finances, local Eclectic "cells" in cities and town throughout the country to maintain correspondence and concerted actions, and a committee to actively communicate with Eclectics in the Armed Forces.

The Navy College Training (V-12) Program joined the Flight Preparatory (V-5) program on campus on July 1, 1943. Four days later the summer term began with 169 civilians and 134 Navy V-12 along with V-5 trainees enrolled. A number of the V-12 students were pledged and initiated into the Fraternity subsequently. Undoubtedly the addition helped Phi Nu Theta through the difficult war years; V-12 members served allotted slots on the Finance Committee of the House. Although Sunday evening sings were abolished,[17] other Fraternity activities probably helped fill the recreational void at the college level. Because of the situation, all intercollegiate athletics, including the "Little Three" competitions, were discontinued for the duration.[18]

Academic standards continued to be emphasized by the Socrats. Ralph Bischoff reminded the brothers of their responsibilities at the regular weekly fraternity meeting of September 29, 1943. The House had not done as well in more recent Jackson Cup competition after the remarkable seven consecutive wins of the late 1930s. Although not falling below third place in 1940 and 1941 and again gaining second place in 1942, the Society was to win only two more first places (1945 and 1946) after the wartime suspension of competition in 1943 and 1944 and before the John Wesley Club began a thirteen-year domination of first place beginning in 1947. Eclectic, with two exceptions, occupied either second or third place, vying with a number of other fraternities. The routine became so established that the Jackson Cup competition was suspended in 1960 by the Board of House presidents and never revived.

Despite the lack of food service in the House, a makeshift snack bar in the pool room provided some opportunity for informal interaction among brothers, especially after Wednesday house meetings. Both the Epistoleus's Report for 1943–44 and Mark Barlow in his reminiscences about the war years mention this break from the pressures of academic endeavors and military training. Mark also recalled that all social activity had not ceased; an outside caterer was brought in to provide at least one formal dinner on house party weekends. As far as residency in the House, he commented, "Because of my age, I did not join the V-12 program until the end of my sophomore year [1943–44]. I lived in the House with no more than half a dozen other civilian brothers. Ralph Bischoff (a *frater in Universitate*) . . . made it possible to keep the House open as best it could. Brothers in the Navy used the unoccupied suites for study during the week and places to sleep on Saturday night."[19] Toward the end of 1943, 146 Eclectics were serving in the Armed Forces according to the count given in the minutes of the Regular Meeting of November 16, 1943.

For the Annual Meetings on June 23–24, 1944, only ten undergraduates and twenty-three alumni were able to attend. The matter of proper terminology in regard to Eclectic and the Socratic Literary Society was still of concern. It was again stated that the undergraduate organization was to be know as "The Eclectic Fraternity."[20] It was understood that "Phi Nu Theta" was an alternate appellation. Pledges were still required to undergo a period of trials. The minutes of July 24, 1944, early in the summer term and shortly after rushing, refer to the office of "slave driver." Brother Delos Aumock Jr. (1947n) had the honor of holding that office. The alumni and undergraduates were careful to maintain close relations. Minutes of August 2, 1944, mention monthly meetings with Socrats and joint monthly "banquets."

The size of delegations in fraternities was a topic of discussion in the fall of 1944. Eclectic sentiment urged a smaller number (thirteen or fewer) than the number eventually approved by the College Senate. The campuswide figure was set at fifteen by the Senate.[21] These later war years were characterized by less chaos and more return to traditional ways, but one can infer the continuing influence of the rapid pace of academic and military life on the Fraternity. Names of initiates were not entered into minutes, as was the general custom before and afterward. Abbreviated literary exercises continued to be the rule: one analysis, one essay, one criticism, and one special topic. Surprisingly, war casualties are mentioned nowhere in the minutes of weekly meetings. The Liquor Committee continued to function but appears to have had few, if any, problems with which to deal. By July 1945, rushing was set for four days, and thirty-seven V-12 members and fifty-six civilians were permitted to rush collegewide. Fraternities were allowed to pledge six civilians each.[22] "Day dates" are mentioned as well as the pledging evening to follow, terms familiar to undergraduates ten years later. All these indications of a slow return to normal routine are contradicted by one significant lacuna. Although there is a place for them, no House meeting minutes appear after August 6, 1945, until October 15, 1947.

Other sources can fill in the blanks,[23] however. According to the *Alumni Record, 1953*, the Navy V-5 Program ended in September 1944 and the V-12 Program in October 1945. Immediately after V-J Day on

September 2, 1945, veterans began returning to the campus. Their presence would leave an imprint on the campus and Fraternity until the end of the decade. By the beginning of the spring term on February 26, 1946, veterans constituted 71 percent of the student enrollment of 508. Many were married, and Clark Hall and the Delta Upsilon house were turned into married quarters to accommodate them initially. Intercollegiate athletic competitions resumed, ushering in an unprecedented era of Wesleyan "Little Three" championships in many sports, including football.

The Fraternity returned to a modicum of normal operations. Erich Fichtner "The Chief" returned to run the dining operation in the fall of 1945, although Kaethe was too ill to join him. The Chief, in coordination with the Thesorauphylax (Treasurer), hired brothers as waiters to help defray their expenses. It was a mark of honor to hold such a position. In the summers, Erich ran the Cottage Inn Restaurant in Old Lyme, Connecticut. Brothers who were often hired as waiters to help him retain fond memories of the experience to this day. The restaurant closed at the end of the decade, principally because of the rerouting of Route 1 away from its site.

Normal literary exercises (two analyses, two essays, two criticisms, and one special topic) were in place by the fall of 1947.[24] A memorial service was held on December 6, 1945, to honor Eclectics killed in the war. Sixteen brothers' names were read out at the service and then included on a bronze tablet placed over the library fireplace of the House on June 21, 1946:

Lt. Eliot M. Newhall (1923), UUSNR
Lt. Charles P. Canham Jr. (1935), USNR
Lt. Roger F. Woodbury (1938), AAC
Lt. Philip B. Harris (1939), USAAC
Cpl. Malcom D. Case (1940), AUS
Lt. Frank B. Johnson (1940), AAC
Lt. George W. Peterson (1940), AAC
Lt. Richard T. Bagg (1941), AAC
A/C Arthur W. Clothier (1941), AAC
Lt. George H. Strobridge (1941), AAC
Lt. James B. Davies, II (1943), AAF

D/C Leroy P. Lawrence (1943), USMS
Lt. William Satterthwaite (1943), USMCR
Pfc. Walker D. Keller (1944), AUS
Ens. Richard Gould (1946), USNR
Lt. Neil B. Rickard (1946), AAF

The Constitution of the Fraternity was amended on the same date in 1946 (Annual Meeting) to allow for the election of associate members of the Fraternity. The qualifications for associate membership were set forth as follows: "persons who are older than college students and are closely associated with the undergraduate fraternity; they need not be graduates of Wesleyan University."[25] This description fit one person. That was Erich Fichtner, "The Chief." He was initiated in a special ceremony on October 23, 1946,[26] the only person ever so honored.[27]

The regular initiation of November 22, 1946, marked resumption of normally sized delegations and traditional events. Fourteen freshman (1950) and two sophomores (1949) joined the ranks of the Fraternity after a sub-rosa supper, the traditional initiation ceremony and signing of the Constitution by each new member, and a banquet with traditional speeches. One short-lived tradition ended about this time according to the November 1946 issue of the *Scroll*. Duke, a Great Dane of mammoth proportions who had arrived as a pup in the spring of 1945, was relegated to a farm in Maryland after terrifying a number of neighbors on and near High Street. House pets never did seem to do very well.

The return of the veterans was not without some problems. The Epistoleus's Report for 1948–49 frankly opined that the vets' return—their age and different outlook—took away from the "organicity" [*sic*] of the House. Mark Barlow struck the same note, but from a different perspective, when he observed, "I returned two years later to anything but a monolithic membership. Most of us had matured and had little patience for the typical fraternity life, desiring only to graduate and get out into the world."[28]

House minutes resume as of October 15, 1947, but an invaluable source of information from the alumni perspective disappears after the Annual SLS Meeting of June 13, 1947. The minutes of subsequent meetings and the reports of chairman of the Board of Directors preserved in well-organized volumes are no longer included in the Socrat box in the Eclectic Collection.[29] As a matter of interest, the minutes of the 1947 Socrat Annual Meeting record that ninety-one members attended, including twenty-five undergraduates. Numbers were definitely back to prewar standards.

One aspect of fraternity life in the late 1940s was a subject of discussion[30] and continued as such for the next twenty years: the blackball system. A number of brothers objected to the *liberum veto* on membership that the blackball system entailed: a single anonymous blackball would automatically reject a potential member. Over time, the rule was relaxed, but until the end of the existence of the Fraternity in its old form, a small number of brothers could exclude a candidate from membership. The Alpha Club again became a prime venue for cultivation of prospective members with more restrictive rules for membership, but others could still join under the new rules (a candidate had to be known by at least one-half of the members and approved by two-thirds of those who knew him).[31]

Another topic of intense debate was the "Charter Gag." The Gag was about the closest the Fraternity ever came to hazing (although line-ups, guttering duty, wakeups, and treasure hunts could be considered close seconds). The origins of the event are murky. The minutes of November 10, 1948, are the first formal reference under that name that I could find, but Michael Fairchild (1969), who experienced it in 1965 and set down an extensive account, wrote that his father, Benjamin T. Fairchild (1935), had been through it in 1931. The elder Fairchild never revealed its existence until his son had been through this rite of passage.[32] Briefly for the uninitiated, the Charter Gag consisted of: (1) an allegation sometime just before initiation that the Fraternity's charter had been stolen, possibly by a pledge or a brother not wanting the pledges to be initiated; (2) a well-acted disintegration of civility in the House among the sophomores, juniors, and seniors; (3) after a somber meeting of the freshmen with the Episteleus (president) and individual sessions with other brothers, a request that the freshmen hold themselves ready for further action; (4) the appearance, in turn, at each pledge's dorm door of a distraught upperclassman with an official-looking envelope containing the "charter" with a request that the pledge return it to the House, but not tell anyone who had "stolen" it; (5) the race to the House and the triumphant entry among the (at first) accusatory, but then jubilant brethren of the "savior" of the house; and (6) the slow realization that it was all a hoax when the "thief" was among those giving heartiest congratulations. The Charter Gag must date from at least the early 1930s, and I suspect it originated in the 1920s — because of the use of the word "gag" and other psychological factors — but I can't prove it.

The gag was the subject of controversy because of its effect on some of the pledges. A minority saw through it immediately and just played along. The majority were taken in (this pledge included), but with the nagging thought that it might be a hoax. Another minority were so taken in that they suffered major trauma when they realized that they had been duped. A pledge in 1950 was so traumatized that the gag was suspended for a year.[33] A slightly revised version was revived thereafter, but I vividly remember a pledge in 1956 fainting dead away when it dawned on him what the real situation was. That incident prompted me to speak with the Chief on the matter and ask his advice. As always, he was a source of great wisdom. He opined that the gag really caused a delegation to coalesce and was fundamentally not harmful. It might leave temporary emotional scars, but certainly not like the physical saber scars left on members of German fraternities. His advice was to keep it.

Singing had always been a Wesleyan and Eclectic tradition. Curtailed during the war years, it experienced a rebirth in the late 1940s, especially with the inauguration in 1949 of the Eclectic Spring Sing, to which the campus was invited. The Mt. Holyoke V-8's and the Wesleyan octet and quartet participated in the first Sing. The enthusiasm generated by the event probably helped lead to the formation in October 1949 of a group initially called "The Idiotic Eight" under the leadership of Dave Moore (1952).[34] The loss of a bass led almost immediately to a renaming of the group as "The Spooky Seven," consisting of Don Burdick (1951) and Thorne Griscom (1952), tenors; Dave Moore (1952) and Dave Gamble (1953), leads; King Berlew (1951) and Dave "Chip" Forden (1952), baritones; and Phil Fox (1950), bass.[35] The name stuck, although the group, known informally as "The Spooks," usually performed as an octet at house parties and other venues. The Spooky Seven were still an integral part of Eclectic into the early 1960s and assisted the House's winning a number of first places in the interfraternity singing competition over the next decade.

Beginning in late 1948, fraternities agreed to assume the expense of accepting three scholarship foreign students a year as members of their dining clubs.[36] The addition of foreign students to the Alpha Club was very popular with most brothers—so much so that in the mid-1950s, the Constitution of the Fraternity was amended as follows:

> The Epistoleus may ask any foreign student in the Alpha Club
> to attend the last two consecutive regular fraternity meetings of
> his eating period. A majority vote shall be sufficient indication of
> the Society's wish in every case. Any foreign student who attends
> a meeting shall be asked to respect its secrecy while attending
> Wesleyan.[37]

As the last predominantly veteran Class of 1949 prepared to graduate, rules of the House were tightened a bit. The senior delegation formed itself into a nominating committee to draw up a slate of nominees for fraternity offices. Nominations, of course, could be made from the floor—and often were. Rules for guttering (see glossary) were clarified: there could be no violent resistance until the victim was out of the dining room—and the call for a member's expulsion had to be for good and sufficient reason.[38] Singing was reemphasized and it was voted to sing the second and third verses of "Phi Nu Theta Floreat" on occasion before meetings. Mimeographed song sheets for instructional purposes were distributed.[39]

Minutes of the Annual Meeting on June 17, 1949, reflect a very good attendance, a huge graduating delegation (twenty-five), and comment that the year had seen the rebirth of a cooperative spirit in the House. Dave "Chip" Forden (1952) observed that he was fortunate to arrive in the fall of 1948 and experience the Delegation of 1949 in their senior year. As veterans of World War II for the most part, they were serious in scholarship and in leadership of every aspect of college life. Men like Frank Wenner contributed to the undefeated record of the football team. Chip mentioned him as well as Randy Brown, Dick Frost, Ernest Inglis, Fran Macy, and Alexander Porter as elder brothers who had a great influence on him and other members of the Eclectic Fraternity and Wesleyan community.[40] We who followed ten years later were told of the "golden era" of the later postwar classes by faculty, administrators, alumni, and older undergraduates who had closer contact with them. They and the Fraternity had survived the war years. They deserve their laurels.

CHAPTER 13

ECLECTIC IN
THE 1950S

odernity imposed itself on Eclectic early in 1949–50. The first mention of the brothers' desire to acquire a television set (or, better, a combination radio/TV/phonograph) appears in the minutes of September 27, 1949. The type of phonograph desired is not specified. If the brothers were forward-thinking, they would have opted for a 45 rpm or even a 33 rpm over the 78 rpm, still common at the time. Continuing the musical tradition, Eclectic hosted the second annual Spring Sing on April 22, 1950, with the Mt. Holyoke V-8's returning and the Connecticut College Shwiffs also representing the fair sex. The Jibers (quartet) and Cardinal Puffs (octet plus one) returned to represent Wesleyan, and for the first time Eclectic's own Spooky Seven performed for a more general audience.[1] Under the leadership of Choragus Dave Moore (1952) the House went on to win first place in the Interfraternity Sing. Needless to say, many a date was impressed as Eclectics broke into song on house party weekends.

The June 1950 issue of the *Scroll* extolls the accomplishments of Phi Nu Theta's athletes. Brothers were active in almost every sport on the campus, both in intercollegiate and intramural settings. The fraternity newsletter also recounts the Chief's plans for a summer return to his native Germany after an absence of seventeen years. Two graduates of the Class of 1949, Sandy Inglis and Frank Wenner, as well as a friend from town (Marshall Prout, Eclectic's milkman), were assigned as chaperones. They were later to be joined by various others in specific locations: Frank Underhill (1941) in Spain, Mike Vinavert (1947) in Paris, and Mark Barlow (1948) in the Alps. Besides making a grand tour, the Chief hoped to visit his eighty-six-year-old mother and several brothers and sisters in Chemnitz in the Soviet Zone of Occupation. He always called his hometown that—never "Karl-Marx-Stadt," the town's name under Soviet occupation and the DDR regime. Some of these grand plans materialized and some didn't, but the Chief made his mark wherever he went.

In the spring of 1951, the question of delayed rushing again became a hot topic. The House suspended regular literary exercises at its April 7, 1951, weekly meeting in order to discuss President Butterfield's proposal for this radical change in rushing procedures. The minutes for that date reflect that the sentiment of the House was against the proposal. Exactly a month later, literary exercises were again suspended for a very active business meeting. The College Body Senate (the new name for the student government organization) had voted a requirement that a first-year student must have a 75 percent average for any marking period prior to being initiated into any fraternity. The new rule evidently evoked considerable discussion, because the House had earlier set its own cutoff at 78 percent.[2] The policy was also established at the meeting on May 7, 1951, that any brother not wishing to say grace before meals should speak to the Epistoleus in order to be excused from the customary rite. Suspension of literary exercises, a rare event, appears to have become more common as the 1960s approached.

The house meeting of May 22, 1951, also witnessed a change in literary exercises that became a tradition. At this last regular meeting that graduating seniors would attend, special topics were given over to the seniors for reflections on their Wesleyan and Eclectic experiences. One of those seniors was David W. "Pete" Peterson, who later became assistant director of admissions at Wesleyan (1954–56) and had a lot to do with admitting us of the late 1950s to the College. Pete responded in considerable detail to my plea for input. Because his comments convey the atmosphere of the Fraternity of that era with great clarity and humor, an extensive extract follows:

> Erich [Fichtner, "the Chief"] and the treasurer kept the books, but the [eating club] operation was part of the house operations. It was a place for brothers needing to save money on food to serve as waiters and dishwashers. And it was a way to invite other students not rushed, to help fill up the dining room and often to look one another over as potential brothers. Immediate rushing was spurned by some of us, but the eating clubs in each house served this purpose well; Wes had *no* central eating facilities then. The

Chief's reputation helped us look over the boys we were interested in. And I, entering WES as a junior, was not interested in fraternity life. My roommate's brother was an Eclectic, he joined at once, insisted that I join the eating club; I got to like the house and brothers, liked the ideal of local control and liberal stance, was flattered that they urged me to join, and I did a few months later. This happened regularly for a small number of brothers each year.

Erich and his wife jointly were in loco parentis during [part of] the war, until her grief at the war deaths of a number of her beloved "sons" deranged her and she was hospitalized by the time I joined in '49. Erich was much beloved by the brothers and served as a father figure when thus approached. He ran a top-notch kitchen and dining room and was a rushing asset in several ways. And his party-after-the-parties, open to the brothers at will, were great fun, with much teasing, singing, shouting and overall camaraderie until the wee hours. He outlasted us all, and still sent up a hearty breakfast the next morning. I am aware there was difficulty with him later and know none of the details, but suspected there must have been misunderstanding on both sides. George Morrill (1942) set up a scholarship at The Chief's death. . . . That money became part of the Literary prizes for the writing program eventually. The Fichtners had a daughter born around 1935. . . . Brothers who worked for him at his summer restaurant in Saybrook knew her.

Table seating required only that one freshman serve his table. Cliques were discouraged and I recall seating as being truly random. House parties required two sittings but this seemed to work smoothly. Always a meal began with a short grace by a freshman (one who offered "a short cheer for God" was at once carried to the showers [i.e., "Guttered"]) and songs started each course and after dessert. Don Burdick (1951) formed all freshmen in '49 and '50 into a singing group and they entertained us often, until initiation at midyear. . . . Faculty guests were at least weekly at supper and oftener at lunch. Everyone enjoyed their presence and they seemed to reciprocate.

Fred Millett was a favorite guest for two reasons; he was always entertaining, and he liked Eclectics, although he was fond of teasing everyone and especially us, probably to keep us from getting a swell head! If he called us "boring" it was likely that the context was that we were never on probation, rowdy, poorly performing, etc. We certainly deserved the title Straight Arrow house and thus the nickname Quiver Club. Other houses razzed us for this, but we took it as envy. And in fact we had our share of bad-actors, but relatively mild in degree and nature. Probably our rushing-time reputation and elegant house resulted in having our pick of new members each year, and [we] chose not to risk adding dead-beats.

Traditions are many, but one always accompanied the party weekend banquet: Someone once found in the cellar a small, darkly tarnished, bent, wobbly, dented, one-handled loving cup, a trophy for some very old and minor competition. We named it the Gribney Cup, for Josiah S. Gribney, a noted, if mythical Socrat roué. We ended the meal by presenting this cup to the female most likely to fulfill the qualifications established for this award, which were never specified to the recipient, but clearly reflected nothing more than the most endowed babe in the room. She was cautioned not to risk bad luck by carrying the Cup home, but to enjoy the honor this weekend and leave the cup for the next party recipient. In my years, Jake Congleton's dates invariably won the award, and deservedly so.

Initiations were always a surprise and relief. The pledges arrived promptly to a dining room hung with many rosebuds across the ceiling, as in "sub-rosa," and sat down with the brothers to a very plain, simple, and small meal in total silence. Pledges were then escorted to the cellar poolroom and pillowcases were placed over each head. And we sat, for quite a while. We were allowed to talk, so we could scare each other with imaginings of the physical abuse we must surely be in line for.

Eventually we were called for, and led blindly up the three long flights of stairs to the Goat Room and lined up before the Kerux (me, one year). As pillowcases came off and wild-haired blinking pledges listened, the Kerux greeted them, all in Latin: "Salvete, avenae, salvete! Sociis in mentis cultura, in cura fraterna, in amicitia sempiterna, in honesta aemulatione, in recto exempio, vobis gratulamur . . ." The group then shuffled to other stations where

they were otherwise addressed, this time in English, about the
fraternity and their obligations thereto. Then they sat through
the literary exercises, the best of the crop, chosen effectively to
scare them witless in anticipation of Their Turn. Then we all sang
"Greetings from our Mystic Union," and descended to the now
elegantly decorated dining room and one of Chief's most mag-
nificent filet mignon feasts, and finally by a welcome from Burton
Camp, senior Eclectic on the faculty, who described the Society
in ways that brought tears to every eye. In closing, we stood and
sang "Tela Mystica," congratulated the new members again, and
sent them home. The entire evening was one of dignity, respect,
affection and maturity.

The ugly brothers ploy was a kind of reaction to the stereo-
type of the straight-arrow, squeaky-clean boy scout image, on
reflection. They were rebelling against this cliché.

Freshmen had to answer the phone, but they found ways to slip
around this at times. One young wag, forced to pick up, addressed
the caller with, "Buckingham Palace, King George speaking." Vic
Butterfield on the other end started to laugh, but by then the
answerer was on his way to the showers.

A custom I enjoyed was the return after a football win. We
gathered in a big circle in the foyer under the chandelier (which
with the Reynolds portrait gone is the only surviving image of
those years) Arm in arm, and belted out WESLEYAN . . . IS E'ER
VICTORIOUS . . . ON THE FOOTBALL FIELD AND TRACK. . . . DO
THE DEED . . . AND WIN THE GLORY . . . AND WE'LL BRING THE
VICTORY BACK. . . . OH RING THE BELLS . . . OF OLD SOUTH
COLLEGE . . . PAINT THE TOWN AS NE'ER BEFORE. . . . LINE
IT OUT, BOYS, PLAY TOGETHER . . . SCORE ONCE MORE, BOYS,
SCORE ONCE MORE . . . over and over again until we were hoarse.
If we sing at all when in the House at reunion time, that's what we
do, under the same chandelier, happily.

The Eclectic song lyrics are the best clues to the true ethos of
the fraternity. Not the table-thumping game songs, nor the Mystic Temple hyperboles we chanted up the stairs linked elephant
style—all of which were fun, but chuckled about. The songs that
had a message: "Tela Mystica" 's summon to a life of service and

"some strength or beauty to it lend" and the initiation song "to our last adopted sons" carrying the message of mutual enhancement. These messages had an impact even as their flowery and phony overstatements were easily ignored. Eclectic men all wanted to pursue of life of meaning and value in the best sense of those words. And most have done so. "Tela Mystica" worked.

In 1950, with many veterans still in the house, interests ran to public affairs, world betterment, government service careers and on campus, the social sciences. But we had artists, musicians, scientists, writers and economics majors too.

Campus media were not attractive except for expression of important ideas. Athletics were very important and most brothers were involved somehow, but not in a career sense.

Concerns? Fixing the leaky roof, even then! Politics were primarily liberal, thanks to charismatic professors and real social needs in a post-world-war-world. Fred Millett used to say, "Wesmen arrive as Republicans, play the Democratic game for four years, and leave as Republicans." I would say few Eclectics left that way; their careers demonstrate otherwise. [Author's comment: Perhaps this writer is the exception that proves "Peterson's rule" re Republican Eclectics.]

Living in dorms was cheaper and house rooms were often scarce. But Pete Bibeault [house janitor 1942 through the early 1960s] did a loyal and good job, if whiny at times, and the house was very comfortable and convenient, and only occasionally noisy or distracting. We studied!

Our reputation was one of respect from most everyone. We did not come across as rich or preppy or jock-filled or alcoholic or hyper-social or racist or nerdy. And all knew we were not really as straight arrow as was teased about.

College involvement [was] primarily in student government, sports, musical groups, service organizations, and groups connected with major program interests. We did not dominate a given group or project or sport. Eclectic grads however were unusually likely to serve later as campus leaders, in administration, public relations, admissions, deanships, faculty, and other paid positions. We were proud of this recognition, and realized it often helped in recruiting new members. [An extraordinary number of Eclectic graduates (ninety-one as of 1993, per David Potts) have served as Wesleyan Trustees.—Ed.]

Other fraternities: Generally we interacted primarily with the major national houses located nearby, but even there, we often had good friends in our . . . classes, regardless of their house or non-house. Remember, there were 600 undergrads on a campus a fifth the size of the present spread! Vic knew our names, and something good about each of us. What a treasure that was, and how we did treasure it.

Our next door [fraternity] neighbor, Beta, was a sometime victim. Like many other campuses, the song "Lets go down and piss on the Beta House" was sung and acted upon during every party. One winter we put up a catapult on our nicely flat roof, and so did the Betas; we lobbed snowballs back and forth, the icier the better. I'm sure other Delegations will report more colorful highjinks. When we pulled down all the shades at Charter Gag Day, they respected our ploy; the Alpha Delts would even come out and console our distressed freshmen: "If they lock the doors, you can eat here with us."

Our alumni were very supportive; those on the faculty would admonish us from time to time, but we really did not give them any grief by our behavior. Handling finances was their major concern, and house maintenance always a cost issue. Alumni not on campus were treated for what they were; some were popular, interested, supportive and helpful; a few were stodgy, reactionary, disappointed in our lifestyle and values. They usually stayed away, and we were civil but not very warm when they visited. In general the recent Socrats were most warmly treated; the older ones were most apt to criticize and we avoided them. Exception: Jolly old "Aught-aught MacNaughten," class of 1900 of course, was a hoot, and came often.

The Great Change (late '60s) and beyond: [Others] will cover this much more adequately since they were in the middle of it all. My take is a sad combination of factors: the druggy '60's, national violence, admission policy changes, a crumbling house with no money to rehab (a huge problem for all local fraternities), and a lack of real leadership and financial support from Socrats who might have stepped in, as a few did eventually, but too late.

The blackball tradition may have ironically done us in. Yes, we had three boxes in the Goat Room; one filled with white marbles, one with blacks, and one empty with a hole in the top. Two juniors defected over the race issue from Alpha Chi Rho, joined our eating club, and hit it off well with most of us. One was initiated without incident. The other received one no vote, from a senior about to leave us. He admitted the black vote was his. Explanation? "I just can't see him for Eclectic." This man was Chuck Exley, [major] donor . . . [to] the Exley science center. He could have saved Eclectic fifteen years later![3]

With Brother Peterson's tour de force on paper, I probably could write a concluding paragraph and wrap up this chapter, maybe even the whole book, but there are other matters that really need addressing before that happy moment.

In the fall of 1950, Eclectic pledged Terry Julius Hatter Jr. (1954), a freshman from Chicago and an African American. According to several Socrats, Terry was the first of his race to be pledged by any Wesleyan fraternity. He was certainly the first black to be pledged by Eclectic, although William Morrill (1952) recalls an attempt in 1947 or 1948 to pledge another African American, which never came to fruition.[4] The action on Hatter caused a storm among a certain segment of the Socrats. Professor Karl S. Van Dyke (1916), chairman of the Board of Directors of the Socratic Literary Society, at the direction of the Board, sent a letter to all members of the SLS.[5] It set forth the fact that Terry had been pledged and was to be initiated with his delegation in December 1950. The chairman reminded Socrats of the questionnaire sent to them in 1947; 175 had responded and of these a large majority affirmed their belief that undergraduates should make their own decisions as to whom they should pledge. The letter then conceded that "about a quarter of those replying stated that they were opposed to the admission of Negroes" and related that, at the request of a nonresident member of the Board, a meeting of that body held with a wide-ranging discussion of the whole topic as the agenda. The two undergraduate members of the Board stoutly defended the action of the House, insisting that the decision was based strictly on "an appraisal on the basis of [his] character, ability, personality, and adaptability." The undergraduate representatives were surprised at the vehemence of the objection by certain members of the SLS, but the decision was left to the undergraduates to make. Unsaid in the letter was the fact that two "legacies" (sons or grandsons of Eclectics) were not pledged that year.

William A. Morrill (1952), who lived through this turbulent time in the House, gave this account of what transpired:

> I was in the Fraternity when the first African American (Terry Hatter, now a Federal judge in L.A.) was pledged at Eclectic (also the first anywhere on campus). . . . That action taken by the undergraduates over the stinging, sometimes totally bigoted objection of some alumni, who sent some pretty dreadful communications to us, . . . [launched] the Fraternity into some needed new directions, but may also have started to break the strong linkage between undergraduates and alumni. I can recall arguing then . . . that the Fraternity belonged to the undergraduates, not the alumni, a view I continued to hold when the Fraternity as we had known it began to disintegrate in the later 1960s.[6]

A young Socrat, Ted Etherington (1948), later president of Wesleyan, was at Yale Law School at the time, got wind of the actions of his unenlightened colleagues, and issued a challenge: for every person who refused to support Eclectic if Hatter were initiated, he vowed to find ten who would deny support if he were refused initiation.[7] Of course, Terry was initiated. When we, the Delegation of 1959, joined the house five years after the events described, the sense of alienation between the Fraternity and some Socrats persisted. Some would say it never healed. No other African Americans were pledged until after 1958–59, but a number were considered. Thereafter, an increasing number was pledged, and there was no repetition of the distressing events surrounding the pledging of Terry Hatter.

In November 1951 the Fraternity received a letter from the Alpha Theta Chi Fraternity asking Eclectic to join it in forming a new national fraternity.[8] Available records do not reveal what, if any, response was dispatched to the eager suitors. There are undocumented claims that more than one hundred bids from other fraternities were received during Eclectic's first 120 years asking that we join them or that they join us to form a national fraternity. Eclectic had long been resolved to remain a local and firmly defended that decision in a number of pamphlets distributed to prospective pledges.

During these early years of the 1950s a number of familiar themes appear in the records. Minutes of September 26, 1950, reflect the concern of the Epistoleus on the "casualness" which seemed to permeate the House. He called for the creation of an Executive Committee to better coordinate activities and shorten meetings. By the meeting of December 5, 1950, the Epistoleus felt obliged to caution the brothers on sloppy dress at meals and meetings, excessive use of bad language, and bad deportment in the dining room. On the positive side, the Fraternity fielded teams in a number of intramural sports: touch football, basketball, swimming, baseball, track, and softball. Literary exercises ranged over a variety of topics and formats: essays on religion, economics, current events, town/gown relations, and fraternity policies (e.g., votes of censure and absence from meetings) as well as works of original poetry and short stories.

The incidents of absence from meetings were serious enough by the beginning of 1952 that consequences for missed meetings (i.e., suspensions) were formally incorporated into the bylaws.[9] (The controversy over attendance was to find outlet in senior reflections a bit later in the year.) At the same time, new rules for determining residence priorities were voted and approved. As was—and would be—the case, the Epistoleus (equivalent of president) and Thesaurophylax (treasurer) were required to live in the House.

A stated policy of inviting faculty guests every Thursday evening was approved in February 1952;[10] the policy and its attendant pleasures remained in effect for at least ten years. Although competition for the Jackson Cup was muted (at least as far as first place was concerned), the House kept close track of grades throughout the decade. For example, it was announced at the regular house meeting of February 26, 1952, that averages were as follows: seniors, 85.4 percent; juniors, 80.4 percent; sophomores, 79.9 percent; and freshmen, 82.9 percent. There is something to be said for the concept of "sophomore slump."

Senior brothers were excused from mandatory attendance at the weekly meeting of May 13, 1952, in view of comprehensive examinations (except for those with literary exercise duties, who were excused immediately thereafter).[11] The following week, however, seniors were at the fore at the somewhat recently established "senior reflections" meeting. Instead of presenting his remarks orally, Brother John R. Jakobson (1952) voluntarily presented a paper entitled "An Evaluation of the Eclectic Fraternity," which he read to the assembled brethren. Needless to say, it created quite a stir. The following is a précis of Brother Jakobson's essay as summarized by this author fifty-four years after the fact:[12]

The author begins his essay opining that Eclectic is Wesleyan's finest fraternity. It provides a superb social and intellectual outlet for its members. Having said that, he alleges that the institution is mired in "institutional lethargy": it is tradition-bound, narrow-minded, and backward. The same may be said of all fraternities, but Brother Jakobson then asserts that the fraternity system is "inherently evil," an "undemocratic tumor in a democratic society."

The essay is intended as a prod for the Fraternity to improve itself, the fraternity system, and the College with an eye to [delaying?] that inevitable day when fraternities shall be abolished.

The Fraternity is lethargic in a number of ways. Its culture places the weekly meeting is the center of its life, when the meeting should exist for Fraternity, not the other way round. Its culture places loyalty to the Fraternity above loyalty to the College and the importance of the meeting above that of the individual.

The essayist proposes a cure for these perceived ills: humanize the structure, de-emphasize the organized aspects of the Fraternity, and stop believing in "a temple grander, lovelier" and such egotistical pretensions. He sees the current life of the Fraternity as overemphasizing an old-fashioned organization that is anti-Christian and anti-democratic. He prescribes getting rid of that emphasis and thereby becoming more democratic—although he muses that the very idea of a fraternity and of democracy are mutually exclusive. He urges the brothers to do away with unswerving loyalty, come out of their lethargy, and remodel.

This remodeling should include more voluntary activities: attendance at meetings should be strictly voluntary; so should literary exercises. That would get the production of the exercises away from their status as a "consummate chore boring fifty people" and would be a cure for the "unadulterated drivel" produced for the Hall.

The brother realizes that he is taking an extreme position, so proposes a compromise solution: Write what you really feel; volunteer when the muse moves you. To democratize, have a new Epistoleus each semester (rather than for a year) . . . the same for other officers. The Grammateus should take over all correspondence, including that with alumni, freeing the Epistoleus for his role as President of the Fraternity.

On a more general level his prescription is: Don't live in the past; senility will certainly set in if changes aren't made; realize that the fraternity system is archaic and doomed; do away with absurd and pompous ritual; change before it is too late!

[Préciist's note: The essay, written voluntarily as Brother Jakobson's senior reflections on his years in Eclectic obviously caused a stir as they run counter to the sentiments of most Eclectics of those years. The article in the June 1952 issue of the *Scroll* on the fourth annual Spring Sing concluded with the words, "The beer party that followed was also eminently successful. It begins to look as if Eclectic is saddled with yet another tradition and one that is deplorably susceptible to Brother Jakobson's bugaboo, 'institutional lethargy.'"]

The following list of requirements for pledges in September 1952 sounds very familiar: freshman beanies, matches, change, table blessing at the ready, jokes, black books, lineups, running for the phone, and full names and hometowns of delegation mates and all brothers.[13] Although not included in the Eclectic list, the prohibition of anyone but seniors using the "senior walk" across the campus was also serious business. Memory fails as to how many black marks were assigned for such a transgression.

The year 1953 opened on a sad note. Horace B. "Hotsy" Rice (1954n), son of Paul North Rice (1910), grandson of Charles Francis Rice (1872) and grand-nephew of Billy North Rice, had left Wesleyan and transferred to a college in the West; he died of a sudden illness in Colorado.

The news was especially traumatic for Harvey Lerner (1954), his roommate from an earlier year. Harvey recalled a stunt he and Hotsy pulled as freshmen:[14]

> Following the Charter Gag, for which we both fell hook, line, and sinker, we concluded that the upperclassmen were getting entirely too uppity. So, in the dead of night we removed all the large pictures from the walls of the living room and took all the silverware except the soup spoons. We stowed the pictures in Bill Low's basement next door (unbeknownst to him). The silverware went under the bed of a non-Eclectic compatriot in a dorm other than ours.
>
> The brothers ate breakfast, lunch, and dinner with soup spoons—and were left to contemplate soup spoons for the Initiation Banquet with the returning alumni. Paranoia prevailed. What competing enemy fraternity had done this dastardly deed and why? The police were called and everyone was warned that this was no mere prank.
>
> The morning of Initiation the silverware mysteriously reappeared and with it a note indicating the location of the pictures. Hotsy and I watched with interest as the upperclassmen restored the pictures to their original locations—a task too important to be entrusted to freshmen.

Hotsy was certainly a different person from his father, one of the elder statesmen of the Eclectic alumni, the staid college librarian in the mid-1950s, and coauthor in the 1930s of the beginning of this history. This further incident, again related by Harvey Lerner, emphasizes the point:[15]

> In our sophomore year, Bill Teachout (1953) was dorm monitor on the first floor of North College and (Detective) John Hutton (1953) was his roommate. An epidemic of firecracker throwing had broken among the freshmen. Bill and Detective John quelled it, and were wont to boast to the rest of us about how they had discovered and nailed every one of the malefactors.
>
> Hotsy convinced me that their hubris should not go unpunished. So, on a warm dark spring night, we quietly approached North College. We slid by the open window of the Teach-

out/Hutton room at the back of North College where the two were quietly studying, deposited our lit firecrackers in the adjoining hallway and walked quietly away.

As the firecrackers exploded, we heard our guys racing into the hallway with a lot of shouting. It was so simple, so easy, just to walk away. The situation begged for another inspiration, for a *pièce de résistance*—throwing two more firecrackers into the room they had just abandoned! So we slid by the window again, firecrackers in hand.

"There they are, the bastards!" Two forms leaped out of the shadows. We took off, circling around to the front of North College and diagonally down the lawn in front toward the Eclectic House. Detective John grounded me with a flying tackle. I don't know how Bill Teachout got Hotsy, but he got him.

The next day was Saturday. Hotsy and I each had to make morning appointments with Dean Eldridge. Hotsy went first while I was doing my duties as breakfast waiter/washer. He came back dejected. "We're both kicked out for two weeks," he said.

I walked up to South College, rehearsing my arguments against this excessive punishment—particularly on behalf of Hotsy, who was in some academic trouble and could not afford this. But when I entered his office, what Dean Don had to say was short and sweet: "You are a campus leader. Get rid of your firecrackers." I sat in stunned silence. I almost said, "You mean I'm not kicked out?" but I managed to hold my tongue. So I finally said something like "Yes sir" and left.

It took a while for me to get my bearings. Then I went looking for Hotsy with a wastebasket full of water. But it was no use. He had gone into hiding.

The official "Annals" have a cryptic note in recounting the major events of 1953–54, "May 2 [1954] Undergraduate disturbance interrupts parade of Veterans of Foreign War."[16] Another of Harvey Lerner's reminiscences fleshes out what went on:

1953–54 was of course the year of the Phantom Marching Band that was led by Terry Hatter (1954) in a bathrobe and Genghis

Khan outfit. . . . My impression is that the PMB consisted mainly of assorted Dekes and a sprinkling of others. [It] arose on the spur of the moment to fill in a gap (the lack of a scheduled rally on the Wesleyan campus) the night before a football game at Amherst. In the following spring it was assembled spontaneously to entertain Deke parents shortly before a Patriot's Day parade sponsored by the Veterans of Foreign Wars. The Phantoms marched; the VFW parade came; and with it came many interesting interactions. The police did not care for the scene, and the VFW later claimed in was a communist demonstration. Terry wound up at the police station, and town-gown relations became tender for a while.[17]

At the Annual Meeting of May 19, 1953, members approved a constitutional amendment proposed by the undergraduates. It eliminated the *liberum veto* aspect of the blackball system by establishing a system whereby the House was divided into units of twelve. For each full unit of twelve, one blackball was allowed. That is, if the House counted forty-eight or forty-nine members and forty-five or forty-six voted for a particular candidate and four voted against, the candidate would be elected.[18] The change took some of the sting out of the blackball system, but it did not please everybody. In the Epistoleus's Report at the same meeting, the matter or "legacies" or "born men" received much attention. The issue had been debated at length during the year and the point made again that, although the fact that a pledging candidate had family connections with the Fraternity would be considered, the undergraduates would make the ultimate decision and would decide any candidacy on its merits. The report concluded that the relationship with the Socrats was "fraternal" and not "paternal-filial." Earlier events obviously still rankled.

As I reviewed my notes on the year 1953–54, a unanimous vote of thanks in the minutes of the Regular Meeting of January 26, 1954, caught my eye. Brother Harvey Lerner was acclaimed and thanked effusively "for keeping silence and thereby shortening the meeting considerably." For further background, the reader is invited to review the two lengthy citations on preceding pages.

At the meeting of May 8, 1954, a new prize was established in memory of Horace B. Rice (1954n). It was to be an annual award to a member of the junior delegation "who has demonstrated the most personal progress during his years in Eclectic." The senior delegation was to make the selection. At the Annual Meeting of June 11, 1954, the first award was made to Robert M. Burrer (1955).

Early in 1954–55 a surprise bequest of $16,000 by Mrs. Frederick Davenport, wife of Brother Frederick M. Davenport (1889), allowed the redecoration of the first-floor rooms.[19] Already the previous summer, there had been a significant renovation to the exterior of the House, including a semi-permanent fix of the roof leak problem. Howard B. Matthews (1928), vice president and treasurer of the University and chairman of the SLS Maintenance Committee, oversaw both projects. The wonderful oriental rugs and comfortable clublike atmosphere in a renovated building that we enjoyed in the late 1950s dated from this period.

In September 1955, undergraduates numbered 774 and tuition was $650[20] as the stellar Delegation of 1959 entered into pledgedom in Phi Nu Theta. The trials we went through to achieve brotherhood have been pretty well described. Two of the sixteen of us claimed they were not fooled into believing in the Charter Gag, but I wonder. The senior delegation were like unto gods, but I suppose most freshmen viewed their senior brothers with awe. Spud Parker (1956) was the Epistoleus for most of the year, and he ran a tight ship. The brotherhood was urged to treat guests in the House with courtesy and warmth, to participate in fraternity and college activities ("You get what you give"), to join in the singing with gusto, to be on time for meals, and to refrain from borrowing other brothers' magazines from the mail table. We freshmen were specifically cautioned to take mail and cleaning duties seriously.

Beginning in the fall term of 1956, the new provision of the Constitution permitting foreign exchange scholars to be invited to the last two meetings of their eating period was put into effect. Philippe Michelot (France) was the first;[21] Ted Morgenstern (Germany),[22] Martin Lenzlinger (Switzerland), Lars Knudsen (Denmark), and others followed during the next few years. In the same vein, there was considerable discussion about loosening the requirement for secrecy concerning literary exercises. A committee established to look into the matter[23] reported its recommendations to the meeting of May 7, 1957. The proposed amendment to the Constitution allowing release of selected essays and so on to other fraternities on request was rather complex; after much debate it was rejected by a two-thirds majority. An even more general proposal to allow discussion in public of the fact that we had literary exercises was defeated nineteen ayes to thirty-two nays. (The idea had been raised in the councils of the Socrats in the 1930s but had not been pursued.) The fact—and substance—of literary exercises was to remain officially secret until the whole subject became moot in the Great Change of the late 1960s. An echo of the policy of so many years still remains in 2006. The Eclectic Repository of literary exercises, resident in the Special Collections in Olin Library since being rescued from the Goat Room, is to remain officially restricted to members only until 2016.

The lack of consensus in the House on this matter of secrecy was symptomatic of a deeper divide in the House in the years 1956–58. John A. H. Briscoe (1959), Epistoleus 1958–59, lay the blame on those who stressed the primacy of individual rather than the welfare of the group.[24] Others saw it as more a division between scholars and athletes ("mooks" and "jocks," in the college vernacular of the day) or between those who took the stated core values of the Fraternity seriously and those who viewed the House more as a place to party. The lack of unity was particularly evident in the Delegation of 1958. Still, with tensions occasionally running high, the situation could be put to positive use in an incident that occurred in 1956–57. The *Argus*, the college newspaper, ran an interview with Professor Fred Millett. In it he commented to the effect that, although Eclectics were individually rather bright and good students, as a group they suffered from bland uniformity and were somewhat boring. That was a challenge!

Inviting faculty members to dinner on Thursday evenings was still very much a custom. Professor Millett was immediately invited to join us the next week. The choreography of the meal was truly wonderful. The athletes sat at one table, wearing the obligatory jacket (the worst anyone could find) and tie—over dirty T-shirts. The raucous noises and food fights emanating from that table would normally have resulted in a mass guttering. The musicians sat at another table: Dave Spencer (1957) honored the assembled with a lovely violin solo, and a member of the Glee Club gave a very credible rendition of "Nessun' dorma." The aesthetes formed another table and several members gave spontaneous readings of original poetry, and on it went. Fred was duly impressed, and, as I recall, apologized to the brethren in a most witty way. The production served as a kind of "safety valve" and tensions were markedly lessened—at least for a time.

All during these years, seniors and juniors were assigned as "big brothers" to freshman pledges. The upperclassmen were charged with helping their "little brother" with adjusting to college life and generally being a friend and adviser. Academics continued to be a concern of the Fraternity, and careful records were compiled of class averages—and particularly of individual freshmen's grades. The idea was to catch problems early and render immediate assistance. Some pressure was taken off freshmen by a decision of the College Body Senate to reduce the grade required of first-year pledges for initiation from 75 percent to 70 percent.[25] As I recall, there was opposition in the House to adopting the new rule, but in the end the membership decided to follow the campuswide policy.

Another feature of Eclectic for many years was the existence of a loan fund, established by the SLS and administered by its resident directors. Needy brothers could apply for a loan, and, if it was justified, receive modest amounts to tide them over. It was a considered a duty to repay, and most loans were indeed repaid. In the 1960s, one of the early signs of changing mores was the rising number of unrepaid loans. But that is a topic for the next chapter.

The minutes of February 4, 1958, report that a motion to form a committee to examine relations with the Chief was approved. The division in the House in the year 1957–58 extended to attitudes toward Erich Fichtner. Not all undergraduates thought of him with respect and fondness. Some disliked the food he served, believed he overcharged, and were suspicious of his motives. There were even accusations that he was accepting kickbacks from suppliers. The report was presented two weeks later with Brother Erich Fichtner (associate member) in attendance.[26] I well remember the meeting. The Chief wore his key and spoke with great emotion about his affection for the House and his philosophy of life. He asked that anybody who had complaints should speak to him personally, either as individuals or as a group. He then said that for the first time in all his years at Eclectic, food was being taken from his storage refrigerators. If the brothers needed snacks in the evenings, he said, he would be happy to leave food out. After shocked silence, a number of brothers stood to speak in defense of the Chief and to condemn any thefts. The report of the committee was accepted, although its contents were not reported in the minutes. After this catharsis, relations with the Chief improved for the rest of the year now and certainly were excellent the following year (1958–59).

In the summer of 1958, the Chief went to Europe again, chaperoned by his newly married daughter Marian and her husband and by Dick Cadigan (1959) and Dick Wenner (1959). For the undergraduate brothers the transatlantic passage was a revelation. The Chief was the life of the party wherever he went on board the ship. They all split up upon arrival in Europe, but both brothers remember the experience with great fondness.

In late February, the Fraternity approved an amendment to the by-laws by which the Epistoleus could invite, from time to time, graduates (i.e., Socrats) to contribute to literary exercises.[27] The practice proved popular, although not invoked more than two or three times a year. I remember Brother Jack Paton (1949), director of public relations for Wesleyan and a former journalist, addressing the House on the craft of writing. Others spoke or wrote on their varied experiences. The practice helped heal to some extent the still-enduring rift between Socrats and undergraduates.

The end of the year 1958–59 saw a number of additional developments. The issue of mandatory attendance at house meetings and the penalty of censure for failure to observe the rule was very much a question. A motion to study the policy was defeated.[28] The issue would be revived a few years later, however. In response to a collegewide questionnaire in May 1959, the Epistoleus, Brother Allan Wulff (1960), responded that there were no discriminatory practices at Eclectic.[29] He was correct. The issue had been decided definitively on the racial aspect during the Terry Hatter matter in the early 1950s. The issue on other historical bases—exclusion on the basis of Jewish or Roman Catholic religious preference—had been decided long before.[30] Eclectic did not exclude from membership on such grounds.

The minutes of May 19 report that as a result of the success of Eclectic's baseball team, the House won the Intramural Athletic Cup. Literary exercises consisted of the sixteen members of the Delegation of

1959 giving their reflections on their time at Wesleyan and in the Fraternity. All related what a great experience both had been. I remember the general outline of my concluding remarks. Although I had not read Brother Jakobson's essay, summarized earlier in this chapter, I agreed with him on some points. I believed that the organization had a wonderful serious core as well as an enviable history and that it deserved to be preserved for future generations. In order to accomplish that, change would have to come. To adapt to the inevitable restoration of coeducation at Wesleyan (or coordinate education with a sister school for women on the Long Lane property), the undergraduates and SLS should soon consider the idea of admitting women. Further, I believed it would be prudent to offer associate membership to congenial graduate students and faculty. This might mitigate some of the antipathy to fraternities that was becoming more evident, especially among younger faculty members. Last, I urged revision of the initiation ritual to eliminate the Latin, which practically nobody studied or understood any more, and translate its meaning along with the existing English passages into more contemporary but still dignified English. If my recollection is accurate, there was a gasp from the assembled brethren. As an self-described monarchist (albeit of the Republican persuasion), I was not known as the most liberal seeker of change in the House.

As I review my notes for these years, a few topics still need to be addressed. The Delegation of 1959 was "eclectic" (or diverse) in one sense, but we tried to be unified in another—to correct the real or perceived failings of previous delegations. In our junior year, we went on a delegation weekend trip to New York City. We had a grand time, although some experiences were grander—or more educational—than others. We also decided as a delegation to room in the House in our senior year, a sacrifice for some who had been RAs (resident advisers) with free room in return for dorm adviser status. It worked. Despite Ted Williams's attempt at flight out a second-story window and his roommates' venture into fermenting apple wine and brewing beer (with sometimes explosive results), we had a positive influence, I hope.

Besides house party weekends, we of the 1950s had lots of diversions. There was Ping-Pong on the porch, an activity of long standing.[31] Also we had slo-mo football on the carpets in the living room as well as outdoors, rug golf, bridge, and pool. One last diversion I must relate.

In 1957–58, some technologically advanced brothers allegedly decided to "bug" the ladies' room (toilet and powder room) on a house party Saturday night. The secret microphone was wired to a tape recorder on a timer. The playback took place on the following Monday evening to the select group "in" on the caper. According to anonymous sources, the tape was stopped after only a few minutes. The attending brothers could not abide the language, content, or comparisons shared by the female guests, supposedly in confidence. There was a lesson there.

The 1950s were a kind of golden age. Many would not say the same of the decade that followed.

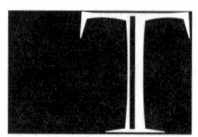he decade got off to a good start. The incoming slate of officers for the year 1959–60, headed by Epistoleus Alan Wulff (1960), continued the practice of using an Executive Committee to clarify issues and set an agenda for weekly meetings. Motions had to be vetted by the committee prior to presentation at meetings, although the rule could be suspended for good and sufficient reason.[1] This arrangement help cut meeting time, always a consideration in the House, and a growing one. The campuswide issue of delayed rushing was very much in the air. A "Woodbury Report," issued in late 1958, urged that rushing be delayed until at least midyear for freshmen. The implications, financial and otherwise, of such a move were disturbing for all fraternities. An undergraduate referendum later in the year opposed proposals for deferred rushing.[2] The same issue of the *Argus*[3] that gave details of the "Woodbury Report" also reported the suspension of the Wesleyan Chapter of Alpha Chi Rho by its national headquarters for tampering with prescribed ritual. The Chapter under the leadership of Doug Bennet ('59), later president of Wesleyan, reformulated itself as the "Black Walnut Club" and later as EQV (Esse Quam Videri—"To be rather than to seem") in protest against restrictive language in ritual and practice of the national organization. Later, in 1959–60 Sigma Chi withdrew from its national affiliation and resumed its old name of "Commons Club"; Sigma Nu did the same, renaming itself as a local "Kappa Nu Kappa."[4] Fraternities were more and more being challenged on their discriminatory practices—mainly against blacks and Jews—and at Wesleyan, they reacted.

Within Eclectic such practices had long since disappeared; the reaction in the House was against internal traditions that grated on some. For a number of years, attendance at regular weekly meetings had been mandatory unless an excuse for just cause was obtained from the Epistoleus. Censure was the normal punishment for violation of this provision of the bylaws. A freshman rose in a March 1959 meeting to move that a committee be established to examine the whole matter of compulsory attendance at meetings and the censure system.[5] The motion was defeated, but signs of a desire for change were in the air.

One externally imposed change had affected the ability of the alumni to raise money to support the undergraduates. In about 1954, the Internal Revenue Service in an undated letter revoked the tax-exempt status of the Socratic Literary Society, which it had granted in a letter of January 25, 1945. The Socrats' appeals were definitively denied by 1958–59: I remember Karl Van Dyke, chairman of the Socrats' Board of Directors, bemoaning the decision and especially the denial. Contributions to the SLS were no longer tax deductible, and the effect was felt almost immediately. The financial condition of the Fraternity was such that contributions from parents of undergraduates were solicited by the Socrats.[6] With no tax deductions, the appeal was not a great success.

Nevertheless, the Socrats managed to fund some needed upkeep and repair. The upstairs shower room was refurbished, and the minutes of January 5, 1960, reflect that "guttering" would no longer be permitted there. There was no indication whether an alternate site was established for this tradition of long standing. Other traditions continued, such as joint dinners for the undergraduates and local alumni. The Epistoleus (president), now Peter Funk (1961), reminded the brothers at the Regular Meeting of May 10, 1960, of an upcoming "banquet" for the alumni. The Grammateus (Recording Clerk and obviously not a Latin scholar) noted in the minutes that the function was for the "Fratres Enervae" (Fratres in Urbe).[7] Maybe they *were* exhausted from wrestling with financial problems.

For the first time since the war years there was no recording in the minutes of an Annual Meeting of the Fraternity in 1960—and also no copy of the Annual Epistoleus's Report. In the last months of the academic year there was an increasing number of censures of brothers who had missed house meetings with no excuse. Censures were also voted against two brothers for "unbecoming conduct" and slight damage to the House; one of the two was an officer of the Fraternity.[8] These incidents are minor in themselves, but taken together they appear to indicate a trend of more casual attitudes toward traditional norms.

Action by the House at the beginning of 1960–61 lent strength to this view, held by a number of alumni and some undergraduates. A report for the proposed alteration of literary exercises was debated by the House and approved.[9] Henceforth, the exercises would consist of one analysis of an essay, one essay, one criticism, and one special topic. Wartime literary exercises had followed this reduced pattern, but the exigencies of the time and the reduced number of members had argued such a course. The main argument for the renewed reduction in the scope of literary exercises was that they unreasonably prolonged house meetings. The new arrangement also halved the number of times a brother would participate in exercises. When this author heard of the change, he worried that the new arrangement signified an increasing lack of commitment to the House and its core traditions on the part of the undergraduates. That concern grew stronger as the result of a further action of the House in early 1961.

The regular weekly meeting of February 14, 1961, tentatively approved an amendment to Article 7 of the Constitution; this article required members to "attend all meetings of the Society and to discharge all duties devolving upon him unless unavoidably prevented."[10] The amendment would make attendance at meetings voluntary for seniors from after spring break until commencement. Again, there were no minutes of a 1961 Annual Meeting of the Society, which according to the Constitution would have had to approve such an amendment by two-thirds vote of those attending in order for it to become operative. Anecdotal evidence indicates that it was never formally adopted by an Annual Meeting; nevertheless, it was placed into operation immediately.[11]

Although specifics were not included in the minutes, the eating club and the Chief were the topic of discussions at four meetings in the spring of 1961.[12] One can infer that the earlier rift between some undergraduates and Erich Fichtner had again opened. Erich attended the meeting on May 9 and gave a talk on the eating club situation. The following week the House voted on a proposal to change arrangements. Again, no specifics appear in the minutes, but after a long discussion the Fraternity decided that the existing eating club system would continue. At this same meeting on May 16, 1961, the seniors gave the traditional talks on their four years at Wesleyan and in the House. There is no indication in the minutes as to whether any seniors took advantage by absence of their newly established "right" of voluntary attendance.

Another change occurred early the next academic year. Pete Bibeault, for many years the houseman, retired. His responsibilities for cleaning and maintenance were undertaken by two undergraduates.[13] At the same meeting that Pete's retirement was announced, the brothers were urged to take their "big brother" responsibilities seriously vis-à-vis the freshmen. One of those responsibilities was to ensure that pledges got to meet and know the Chief.

The effort to help heal the breach between the Chief and a number of brothers very obviously did not do much good. The minutes of meetings throughout October are full of references to unhappiness with the nature and timing of evening snacks sent up to the dining room by the Chief,[14] the kinds of breakfasts provided,[15] and finally, very explicitly, "the old case of Chief vs. the Eclectic Brotherhood brought before the Court with, as usual, no verdict."[16] At the same meeting, there was reference to the need to restore decorum in the dining room. Apparently, there had been a particularly bad incident involving a guest couple at an evening meal.[17] The Chief himself was the victim of an anonymous letter-writing campaign. In a letter read to the House and recorded in the minutes of October 30, 1961, he expressed outrage at a series of "insulting notes" sent without signatures to him. He included the notes, which were read to the House. The Epistoleus cited them as another symptom of a "downward trend," which also included an incident of beer cans being thrown out of the front windows of the House, laxness on the part of the waiting staff, the "mess" in the Elephant Room (waiters' dining room), and many brothers' failure to wear coat and tie at times when they were prescribed.

One can tell that matters had reached some kind of crisis. Meetings were held on consecutive days at the end of October to discuss the spiraling incidents of unmannerly behavior and gross conduct in the House as well as the refusal of one brother to present his scheduled literary exercise. The Epistoleus, Charles R. Work (1962), reminded the brothers of their initiation oath to uphold house policies and traditions.[18] To address the situation, a committee was appointed to look into the role of censure and the functions of the Liquor Committee. At the next meeting, the committee presented its report and recommended changes to the bylaws—abolishing the Liquor Committee, redefining censure, and establishing a Judicial Committee with wide powers, but subject to appeal to the whole membership. The new Bylaw amendment was passed at the same meeting.[19] The new Judicial Committee began to function immediately under its elected chairman, Lawrence H. Sprouse (1962). The committee presented its first report on November 21, 1961, as recorded in the minutes of that date. The report was approved, and it was noted that the new committee replaced the Liquor Committee, had flexibility in imposing penalties, and considered infractions on a case-by-case basis. One of the infractions considered was the defenestration of some furniture, the first but not the last incidence of this kind of behavior. Literary exercises were canceled for the meeting of November 21, the second time in a row, even though the prior meeting on November 14 included an initiation.

In early December 1961, the Chief announced his retirement at the end of the school year.[20] He had served as chef and unofficial house father since September, 1938, a period of twenty-two years — not counting the two years the Alpha Club was closed during World War II, when he worked in Hartford. In private discussions later with his good friend George Morrill (1942), Erich said that his years in the House were of deep satisfaction to him. He only regretted periods during the last few years when there was estrangement. He opined that the type of personality in the House had changed. It was time to leave.[21]

At the same meeting during which the Chief's upcoming retirement was announced, two major items of business came before the House. The first was the creation of two new offices, steward and vice president. According to the motion, the vice president was to assume the duties of the Grammateus (recording clerk) and some other administrative duties. He was to be elected from the junior delegation.[22] The other major item of business was the presentation of the report of a committee on literary exercises. The latter provoked considerable discussion, and was laid on the table until after the Christmas 1961 break.

According to the minutes of that date, the report on literary exercises was taken up again on January 9, 1962, and accepted, but action on its recommendations awaited a special meeting on the next day. At that meeting, the committee's recommendations were divided into four parts, each of which was approved by the House: (1) penalties for failure to present scheduled exercises; (2) a new method for assigning dates of appointments; (3) a resolution encouraging "literary imagination"; and (4) automatic censure for a brother's failure to attend the literary exercise part of meetings.[23] Although not mentioned in the minutes of this meeting, later references indicate that brothers could now pick their own critics, rather than having them assigned by the Epistoleus.[24] Chuck Work (1962) finished his term of office as Epistoleus with a flurry of activity.

New officers were elected the following week. Lawrence T. Yeo won election as Epistoleus; Thomas A. Spragens Jr. as "Grammateus"; and Bruce W. Miller as Steward.[25] All three were members of the class of 1963. A new office was also created, that of "Alumni Secretary." At the first meeting of the new semester, the new Epistoleus laid out his view of challenges that faced the Fraternity. Specifically they were active participation in house projects by all brothers; finances, especially tightening the budget; house maintenance; cooperation in rushing; dining room and eating club matters in view of the Chief's imminent departure; enhancement of scholarship; stimulation of social life; the intramural athletic program; and relations with alumni.

A continuing problem was the failure of brothers to pay bills owed to the House. In early March 1962, the Fraternity owed $2,000 to creditors, but members owed the organization $2,600 in back dues, room rent, and dining club bills.[26] Although not required to be members of the Alpha Club, Eclectic brothers in increasing numbers opted not to eat at the House. The minutes of February 20, 1962, indicate that those individuals should pay for snacks. Decorum in the dining room and less than cordial welcoming of guests were also problems mentioned in minutes as the academic year came to a close. Two other major issues also presented themselves. One was the shape of dining hall operations the next year—whether it should be a catering service or an independent operation. The second was the issue of secrecy concerning house meetings, particularly literary exercises. The decision on dining hall operations was deferred, and motions to delete the requirement for secrecy from the Constitution, to allow nonmembers to attend meetings at the invitation of the Epistoleus, and to strike all references to a requirement for secrecy from the initiation protocol were all defeated. The departure of the Chief was noted; a party to honor him is mentioned in minutes of May 15, 1962. Again, no minutes for an Annual Meeting of the Eclectic Society appear for the year 1962. It could be that they simply were no longer held, despite a constitutional provision requiring them.

The academic year 1962–63 opened with delayed rushing a fait accompli for the year. The Wesleyan Trustees had issued a statement in February 1961 "enjoining an early change to deferred rushing."[27] In January 1962 the student body reversed its opinion and in a referendum called for fraternity rushing in February freshman year; a month later the Trustees made it official.[28] The physical change that made carrying out this decision possible was the completion of the McConaughy Dining Hall in the Foss Hill Freshman Dormitories. Eclectic and the other fraternities had to carry on with no freshmen regularly in their eating clubs or participating in other fraternity activities, at least during the first semester.

At other colleges, fraternities were under attack by presidents, faculties, boards of trustees, and students opposed to the system. As part of the literary exercises of September 25, 1962, as reflected in the minutes of that date, William P. White III (1964) presented a paper entitled "Deviation," which was stimulated by an article in the *New York Times* on Williams College's abolishing its fraternities and taking over all feeding, housing, and entertaining functions. He related that his brother's fraternity agreed to the move and was to surrender its house. Brother White then turned his attention to the situation in Eclectic. In his view, the need in early days of the Fraternity was for intellectual stimulation, but in the present day the need was for relief from overburdening academics. "Decrepitude" was settling in at Eclectic: house spirit was down; there were problems with the Alpha Club; undergraduates were no longer super-rich; and many had to work in the dining halls in order to get by. Because of academic pressures, there was no time for socializing: "The era of leisure is rapidly fading into the past, and following close on its heels, the era of the fraternity." He noted the decline in the importance of tradition, the "corner stone" of the fraternity system. Specifically in the House, he observed the disappearance of Eclectic traditions. He foresaw a dim future for fraternities at Wesleyan. He predicted that if someone should write in five years (i.e., 1967) about Wesleyan fraternities, that person would be like Thucydides writing about the decay of Athens. Brother White's prescription was to "stop the decay ... vote ourselves out of existence before Eclectic is tainted with the eventual condemnation of all fraternities." Specifically he urged that at the 125th anniversary of the Fraternity (to be marked at a reunion meeting the following month), the assembly should "dissolve the seldom mystic union," turn the building over to the College as a new "Butterfield College," and take over Clark Hall the following year as a place merely to live close to each other.[29]

At the same meeting during which Brother White presented his essay, an item of business was the discussion of the state of literary exercises, including possible substitutes. Furthermore, there was a mention of the campuswide circulation of the Constitution of the Socratic Literary Society, supposedly a confidential document, but circulated as a prank.[30] Traditions certainly were under assault.

The 125th anniversary of the founding of the Eclectic Society of Phi Nu Theta was celebrated at an "Anniversary Reunion" on October 26, 1962. At the house meeting portion of the event, Edward M. Dreyfus (1965) read an essay by Charles L. Bonnell (1868), who lived from 1846 until 1902. The essay, entitled "Dawn of Peace," was written for the Hall in 1865, three weeks after the end of the Civil War.[31] At the same meeting, it was reported to the assembled undergraduates and Socrats by the Epistoleus, Larry T. Yeo (1963), that plans were under way to revitalize the *Scroll*, the newsletter intended for all Eclectics. Brother Yeo also discussed the difficulty of running a three-delegation House, undergraduate reactions to the catering service in the post-Chief era, and satisfaction with the new houseman, Steve Traskus.

The effects of delayed rushing appeared in an entry in the minutes of February 20, 1963. It was announced that freshmen would be eating in the House the following Thursday evening. Continuing problems with attendance at meetings plagued the House in March. Censure motions were brought against seven members, six of whom were censured.[32] The following month, the problem of attendance was still a burning issue. The Judicial Committee adopted a five-point system of penalties again infractions which had been proposed a year and a half earlier by Hank Sprouse (1962). On the same theme, a motion to require seniors to attend initiations was at first tabled,[33] but then discussed and passed.[34]

Although no Annual Meeting minutes again appear in available records, the Epistoleus's Reports for 1962–63 are included in the *Eclec-*

tic Repository. The reports, while optimistic, are frank. The Epistoleus, Richard H. Colton (1964) reported that the outlook for the House was "upbeat" after a period of "doubt and debate," reflected in both attitudes and literary exercises. He noted that Jackson Cup competition (academic excellence among fraternities) had been discontinued in view of new college academic policies that made determining meaningful grade averages well-nigh impossible. Eclectics were very active in many spheres of endeavor on the campus. Despite continuing problems with late payment of house bills, the Thesaurophylax, Bob Berger (1964), had gotten the House back on track financially. Some brothers, however, wanted much from the House, while not wanting to give anything in return. They consider house meetings a burden. Perhaps most disturbing, he observed "the most elementary rules of social responsibility are flouted regularly by Eclectics." [35]

Delayed rushing continued for the second year in 1963–64. According to the *Alumni Record*, the year opened with an undergraduate student body of 1,064, with tuition increased to $1,500.[36] Saturday classes were dropped. In comparison with previous years, minutes of the weekly meetings are very sparse. Those of the meeting of October 22, 1963, indicate that there was concern for too much growth in the number of brothers in the Fraternity. There was discussion of limiting the number of freshmen to be taken into the House after the semester rushing break to twenty, but no decision was apparent in the minutes. At the same meeting, it was moved that smoking be permitted in the Hall during meetings. The motion was defeated. Continuing themes reflected in the 1963–64, minutes include the requirement for jackets and ties at dinner, college faculty and staff invited to dinner on a regular basis, normal practice should be that brothers eat in the Alpha Club (unless "financial necessity" deems it otherwise), a regular "Spring Sing" in April (after the initiation of freshmen), and dining hall troubles (although "Al" was to be retained as chef the next year). The Founders Prize still existed, for it was mentioned in the minutes of May 12, 1964, but no laureates were mentioned, and no Annual Meeting minutes appear to record who won the honor.

Early rushing was restored by the University Board of Trustees for 1964–65.[37] A strong Delegation of 1968 was pledged under the revived rule. A Mr. Keller was selected to serve as Steward and to do all the buying and serving for the Alpha Club.[38] At the same meeting it was noted that poor attendance at meeting continued to be a problem—to the extent that a vote on membership had to be postponed. Nevertheless, initiation was held on December 11, 1964, with Jack Hoy (1955) as principal speaker. The Charter Gag was played on the freshmen two days before the date of initiation. Initiates were not required to buy a fraternity key (never a requirement in recent years). The price was quoted as $27.80 per golden scroll key.

Pericles still guarded the inside front door, for the minutes of January 5, 1965, indicate that his bust was to be repaired to its condition "before the fall." For a number of years in the 1950s and perhaps later, one of the duties of the youngest Delegation was to prevent the kidnapping of Pericles by members of other houses, most prominently Psi Upsilon. The marble bust weighed nearly 200 pounds and was no easy piece to lift. It probably was damaged in one of these scuffles. In 1955, the Delegation of 1959 had rigged an elaborate alarm system to prevent a theft. It worked, but only to awaken sleeping brethren on the second floor. It was disabled when the real test came. It took a few days to get Pericles back from Psi U.

In February 1965 Gary B. Conger (1966) was elected Epistoleus, replacing Thomas E. Dardani (1965). The minutes of February 2, 1965, mention both the term "Epistoleus" and "president," but with increasing frequency English terms are used for the officers of the Fraternity. The same minutes also mention that there was a cook as well as Mr. Keller (the steward) in the kitchen. The question of the "right" of seniors to be excused from mandatory attendance at house meetings was raised again later in the month. A motion was made that seniors be excused after semester break. The motion did not carry, but the point was made that the pressure of writing senior theses was a valid excuse for being excused from meetings.[39] In March 1965, freshmen were assigned special topics to get them involved in literary exercises.[40]

In March and April 1965 unauthorized absence from and lateness to meetings was a continuing problem. New penalties including censure for two unauthorized absences and a fine of five dollars per censure were approved. At the earlier of the two meeting, the contents of a letter from Middletown authorities were made known. The letter stated that there was an urgent need for improvement in sanitary conditions in the kitchen.[41] In mid-April the departure of "Al" the cook at the end of the school year was announced. At the same meeting, Larry Cody was made "an honorary brother."[42] Mr. Cody, who was not further identified, does not appear in any Wesleyan alumni record. According to Amendment 2, Section 3, of the Fraternity's Constitution, which was still in effect, honorary members could be elected only at an Annual Meeting of the Society after having been proposed at the previous Annual Meeting. Election had to be unanimous. Associate members, authorized by a constitutional amendment in 1946 to accommodate the membership of Erich Fichtner, also had to be elected unanimously at an Annual Meeting, but without the requirement for a year's postponement. The last meeting 1964–65 was held on May 18. The minutes reflect that the seniors gave their talks and that the Founders Prize still existed, but no selection was indicated and, again, there was no indication of any Annual Meeting to be held. Again it appears that the Constitution was simply ignored.

The academic year 1965–66 began with a number of traditions still in place. Minutes discuss invitations to faculty to lunch, scheduling the Charter Gag, initiation, and coats and ties required at dinner. Literary exercises evidently did not enjoy the respect among many brothers that they once had. An entry in the minutes for November 13, 1965, characterized the meeting as "dump on literary exercise night."

The last book of minutes for the Society in its old form begins with entries for the weekly meeting of January 11, 1966. No further entries appear after what was undoubtedly June 6, 1970, (the last few minutes were undated, but references allowed a fairly sure fixing of the date). The appearance of the book itself tells a story. Pages are stained with some kind of spilled liquid and entries are often very difficult to read. Election of officers occurred on February 1, 1966. Greek titles appeared again with the mention of Charles J. "Mike" Cronan (1967) as the new Epistoleus and C. Stephen Keim (1967) as the relieving Thesaurophylax. English titles were used for the vice president elect, Harry M. Shallcross (1967), and steward, Robert W. Day (1968). The annual Alumni Dinners in New York were still being held, for the minutes of March 15, 1966, mention that the event was to take place on April 11. They were discontinued the next year. At the same meeting, the existing policy of asking faculty members to lunch was reaffirmed and a new policy of asking faculty to present papers in the Hall was instituted. There is no mention of the latter having to be Eclectics. Both policies were intended to strengthen faculty/member relations.

Instability in eating club arrangements continued to plague the House. It was announced at the April 5, 1966, meeting that Mr. Keller had left Eclectic. "Ray H."[43] was now doing the buying. The first in a series of reports of brothers going inactive was given at the April 5 meeting. A member of the Class of 1970 and one from the Class of 1967 notified the Fraternity that they wished to be considered in an inactive status. On the brighter side, it was announced that a bill owed the House since 1959 had been paid.

Lack of interest in living in the House and a proposal (tabled) to conduct literary exercises in a voluntary Sunday evening meeting open to all brothers, faculty, and invited guests—which would excuse brother from the Tuesday evening meeting—were all discussed at a mid–April 1966 meeting.[44] Change was more and more in the air. One tradition continued into this year; the members voted to award the Founders Prize to Gary B. Conger (1966) and Joel B. Russ (1966).[45] Another tradition was slightly modified, in that two—rather than one—Annual Reports appear in the *Eclectic Repository*. The spring report delivered by Epistoleus Mike Cronan (1967) addressed the difficult environment with candor. The president and dean were quoted as saying, "The fraternities must either fulfill their role in the community or perish." Brother Cronan then commented that neither indicated exactly what that role should be. He further commented that the Fraternity should not do certain things just to please the powers-that-be but should do things because they are appropriate and the brothers want to. He opined that tensions in the House arose principally from the competing principles of individuality and house unity. The alumni were being supportive, Jack Hoy (1955), then Wesleyan Dean of Admissions, being specifically mentioned in that context. A second report was delivered on June 3, 1966, evidently to the SLS. It outlined the main events of the year: reinstitution of immediate rushing, a strong freshman delegation of twenty members, increased functions to foster student/faculty rapport, and active involvement in campus activities by many brothers. Problems mentioned included the storm of internal criticism raised by members during the year, the challenge of competition from the University in provision of living and dining facilities, and the general atmosphere of protest and antiestablishment rage created by the Vietnam War. Unmentioned in the Report was the matter of rising use of illegal drugs on campuses, specifically at Wesleyan and in the House.

Brother Cronan did address drug use and the University's policy toward it at a weekly meeting early the next year.[46] Other matters of concern are evident in the minutes throughout 1966–67: brothers going inactive voluntarily or as a result of suspension for violation of rules, the lack of proper dress at meetings, late payment or even nonpayment of house bills and resulting in cash insolvency and ever-increasing fines for late payment of bills, increasing censures (as many as seven or eight a week) and serious dissatisfaction with the shape of literary exercises, including one case of absolute refusal by one brother, an officer of the Fraternity, to give his assigned presentation. The earlier proposal to have open literary exercises once a month with no business to be conducted was approved and put into effect. The first such exercise recorded in the minutes occurred on April 18, 1967, with Professor George Creeger reading an essay on Truman Capote's *In Cold Blood* together with a regular undergraduate essay, read and critiqued. Another evident effort to enliven literary exercises took place earlier in the year. The minutes of November 1, 1966, indicate that an essay entitled "Promotion for Murder" written by Brother Edwin D. "Ted" Etherington (1948) as an undergraduate and the associated contemporary criticism were read at the meeting. The reading may have had a different impact than was intended.[47]

Another honorary brother, a Tomas Oliva, was initiated on December 2, 1966, according to the minutes of that date. Again, the Constitutional provision for election by an Annual Meeting was not observed. A further, lighter indication of some disorder in the House, especially among residents, may have been the creation of the office of "Zookeeper" in the slate of officers nominated for election by the seniors on February 7, 1967. The slate was approved at the next two meetings, and William H. Redkey (1968) was elected Epistoleus/president. The Socrats were still supporting the House financially. They funded a redecoration of the living room in time for a symposium held on the Vietnam War.

Brother Redkey's two reports as Epistoleus followed the pattern of the previous year. The first was delivered to the House on February 6,

1967. It stressed that there was a need to "foster healthier house attitudes." He mentioned the problem of brothers going inactive, but noted that other fraternities had the same problem, to an even greater degree than Eclectic. His suggested solutions to the problem were more involvement by brothers in house functions and activities and the constitution of a larger executive committee to encourage more participation in the business of the House. The second was delivered to the Annual Meeting recorded in the minutes of June 2, 1967. It noted the comment by many returning Socrats that the House had changed a great deal since they were undergraduates. Brother Redkey then commented that change was inevitable but that the undergraduates needed to know what had gone on before. He then addressed the sea change within the University: the critical attitude toward fraternities and the assumption that they would die out; the decreasing number of students pledging fraternities from year to year;[48] the decrease in fraternity size [Eclectic's from eighty (in 1964) to sixty (in 1967)]; and fraternity members'—including Eclectic—willingness to leave fraternities over dissatisfaction. Many of the same themes already mentioned in 1966–67 appear in the Epistoleus's Report, but he sounded a positive note with reference to the brothers' involvement with charity volunteer activities, campus activities and athletics, and improvements to the physical plant (living room, bathroom, recreation room progress). Still, the poor attitude on the part of many brothers toward accepting responsibility—especially in regard to financial obligation to the House and despite punitive measures—needed attention.

The next two years, 1967–68 and 1968–69, marked a further decline in observance of traditions and traditional norms in the Society. The last bound volume in the Eclectic Repository was put together for the year 1963–64; a few loose essays through 1968 are included in a box held in the Olin Archives, but large gaps appear. Literary exercises continued sporadically, but it appears there was no attempt after 1968 to preserve them, as was required by the Constitution. Another motion to have smoking permitted at meetings was made at the meeting of October 24, 1967. It was referred to the Executive Committee with the Grammateus's marginal comment, "presumably tobacco only";[49] the motion was defeated when reported out of Executive Committee on November 7, 1967. A formal initiation of the Delegation of 1971 was held in December 1967. It was the last. If any were held thereafter, they did not follow the requirement in the Constitution that members sign the Constitution (sometimes interpreted as the minutes).[50]

Beginning in January 1969, the language in the minutes and the quality of its coverage of fraternity proceedings deteriorate markedly. Dates of meetings are often omitted, and only words or phrases, written illegibly, are increasingly the only record of Society proceedings. New officers were elected and recorded, however, on February 6, 1968, including the "president" (Greek titles disappear completely), Daulton J. Lewis (1969). He obviously was frustrated by the task he inherited. At a house meeting of mid-April, he set forth the following statement of his policy, phrased in the third person to emphasize that he was speaking in his role as president: "Unless the brotherhood begins to show that they do, in fact, desire to remain as a fraternity, he will decline to fulfill organizational responsibilities beyond the absolute minimum required by the office." The following discussion centered around the "malaise" afflicting the House.[51] For the rest of 1967–68, discussions centered around what to do: make the house a dorm; turn it over to the University; make it a coffeehouse. No decisions were taken, and the House continued in theory on into 1968–69.

Michael M. Fairchild (1969) responded to my plea for input for the writing of this history. He wrote a wonderfully entertaining description of his experience in 1965 with the Charter Gag. He also reflected on the changes that occurred in the House. His remarks are well worth quoting:

> I graduated in 1969 from Wesleyan and I was also Vice President of Eclectic my senior year. My father, Benjamin Fairchild, was an Eclectic who graduated in 1935. I was witness to a sharp decline in the academic and institutional quality of life at Eclectic in the fall of 1968 and the spring of 1969. The brothers didn't want to bother with the traditions like the literary exercises or the annual sub rosa dinner [associated with initiation] which I had enjoyed so much my first three years. A warm, supportive atmosphere in the House changed to a sloppy, sometimes hostile scene. . . . During my last year, I moved out of Eclectic to [the] Lawn Avenue dorms for a more quiet environment.[52]

Minutes in the last book of minutes continue into 1970 but are sporadic, in pencil, and mostly illegible. Earlier entries (1968–69) indicate that literary exercises continued on an ad hoc basis, but no copies survived in materials available in the archives. After a four-month gap between November 19, 1969, and April 1, 1970, the last reasonably full entry covers the meeting of May 10, 1970, but only a few squiggly lines scratched on (what one must deduce was) June 6, 1970, are evidently intended to convey what went on that last day. If one had to assign a date to the end of the old Eclectic, I suppose June 6, 1970, would be as good as any. The fuzziness at the end certainly balances the fuzziness at the beginning, when even the first members and their immediate successors couldn't agree on the exact point of founding.

EPILOGUE

The year 1970 marks the end of the old Eclectic for another reason. That is the year that the Socratic Literary Society sold the House at 200 High Street to the University. Discussion concerning the future of the physical plant had been going on among the undergraduates since at least 1968, as mentioned in the previous chapter. The first specific reference to a proposal to sell the House in available Socrat documents[1] is in an enclosure to a memo dated April 11, 1969, from James E. McCabe (1939), member of the Committee of the Future of Eclectic, to John R. Corkran (1958), chairman of the SLS Board of Directors 1968–69. The enclosure, dated April 9, 1969, is addressed to Donald C. Bruster (1948), an Eclectic and vice president for business affairs of the University, from David B. Jenkins (1953), a member of the Board of Directors and chairman of the Committee on the Future of Eclectic. The enclosure formally proposed a sale of the building to the University with a leaseback to the Fraternity. In a handwritten reply dated May 10, 1969, Brother Bruster gave the University's reply. It basically agreed to the idea of a sale/lease-back arrangement, but with many details to be worked out.

The sale (alternatively gift)/leaseback idea along with two very different proposals was discussed at the Annual Meeting of the Socratic Literary Society on June 6, 1969. The second alternative proposal was to continue operations as they were and to conduct a capital campaign to raise $100,000 to bring the House living and dining facilities up to university standards. The third alternative proposal was to dissolve the Fraternity and donate the building and other resources to the University for its use with the proviso that they should be used for purposes consistent with the objects of the fraternity (e.g., establishment of a literary college, offices for visiting faculty, or headquarters for graduate students in the humanities)—or sale of the building to the University without restriction with the resulting funds to be devoted to purposes in consonance with the objects of the Fraternity (e.g., special scholarships, teaching incentive grants, stipends, or lecture programs). Option 3 (dissolution) gained a fair amount of support, along with option 1 (sale/leaseback). Option 2 (capital campaign) received almost no support. According to the call for a special meeting of the SLS set for September 27, 1969, the Annual Meeting directed the chairman of the Board of Directors for the year 1969–70, Lee Allison (1955), to appoint a committee to negotiate a definitive sale/leaseback agreement for approval by the Society and presentation to the Wesleyan Board of Trustees at their October meeting. A postcard mailed to Socrats on October 30, 1969, reported that the meeting of three days before had received overwhelming approval but that the Wesleyan Board had voted to defer action on the plan until its December meeting. The delay resulted from the Trustees' concern over the status of fraternities in general and Eclectic in particular and their fear that many other houses would follow suit if the Trustees accepted the Eclectic plan, thereby tying up a lot of university cash with no income.

The deal was finally struck and papers signed on July 7, 1970,[2] and based on the following: The House, the land, all its furnishings, and the endowment fund (estimated at $90,000 to $95,000) were given to Wesleyan. The Socrats would lease back the facility (except the lower back yard) for the sole use of Eclectic. In return, the University would refurbish and update the facility to a level comparable to the dormitories, renovation to start "as soon as possible"; credit income from the endowment fund, regular room rentals, and summer use toward the lease; and cancel the outstanding loan from the University to the Fraternity in the amount of $10,000. Further, the University would assume responsibility for full maintenance (except the interior of the meeting room). The Socrats agreed to make up any difference between income generated and the cost of the lease up to $3,000 per year for the first ten years of the lease. The lease was to run as long as it was not defaulted. Other minor provisions also pertained.[3] Work on the refurbishment of the House was delayed until September 1970 for various reasons, so the members were obliged to move into the Beta Theta Pi House, which had suspended operations for a year.[4] Another brother, George Withey (1945), was in charge of the refurbishment project for the College, but the delay in completion was blamed on the University negotiator, Brother Don Bruster (1948). He reflected on the imbroglio as follows:

As with many construction contracts, the deadline was not met by the contractor, and the Eclectic members became very agitated with the delay, with the result that I was "hanged in effigy" from the Beta House second story with a large sign reading "Bruster, Honkey Slum Lord." This did not speed up completion, but it did give a lot of people a laugh, including me.[5]

The Babylonian Captivity lasted until April 1971.

Another sad event also marked the end of the old Eclectic in an emotional sense. Word was received in January 1970 that the Chief, Brother Erich Fichtner, and his wife Kaethe had been found dead on January 14, 1970, in their vacation rental in Fuengirola near Malaga, Spain. The exact circumstances of their deaths were unclear at first, but rumors that they had died a considerable time before their bodies were discovered appear not to be true. According to Marian, their daughter, the two had been traveling in Europe visiting relatives and enjoying full retirement. The weather on the Continent had been very cold and they decided to rent a place in Fuengirola on the Costa del Sol, normally temperate even in winter. Kaethe's brother from Germany came to visit and found that even sunny Spain was uncomfortably frigid. The houses generally had no central heating and during such unusual cold snaps natives and tourists alike would depend on small gas space heaters. The Fichtners were using theirs when Kaethe's brother left. According to a number of sources (and personal experience) the devices were notoriously fickle. The flame could go out and the emergency gas shut-off would malfunction with alarming regularity. That is what evidently happened to the couple during the night of January 11 or 12. They were discovered two to three days later and initially interred in Fuengirola. Eventually their ashes were returned to the United States, where they now rest in the Mt. Auburn Cemetery in Cambridge, Massachusetts.[6]

A memorial fund was set up in March 1971 to honor the Chief and Kaethe. George Morrill (1942), their old friend, acted as custodian.[7] After several alternatives were considered, it was decided to award "The Chief's Prize" to the member, chosen by the undergraduate brotherhood, who "best exemplified throughout the year the Chief's characteristics of humanity, generosity, and hospitality." At least one award was made—to Ray Hoagland, the Chief's eventual successor as chef.[8]

After a time, the money in the fund was turned over to the University for a prize to honor literary accomplishments.

THE END OF THE OLD ECLECTIC: WHY?

A number of Socrats who had a close connection with the undergraduate society in the 1960s commented that the Fraternity changed from its traditional shape to something quite different within the space of two years, 1967 through 1968.[9] There is no doubt that those years witnessed an accelerated pace of change, but this author would argue that the transformation (some call it the decline and fall) of Eclectic actually started well before those two years. A healthy critical view of the Society coupled with a willingness to express such views had always been a hallmark of the Fraternity. As early as 1848, as recounted in chapter 2, two members left, with one criticizing the organization very explicitly. Essays in the literary exercises through the decades appeared with frank analyses of perceived institutional deficiencies. Two in particular are summarized in earlier chapters dealing with the 1950s and the 1960s (earlier part). When a healthy minority attitude became a majority attitude (approaching self-hatred), the Fraternity was in deep trouble. Minutes of the late 1960s reflect such a development; a significant number of members lost faith in the positive value of the institution.

Debates over the primacy of the individual versus the ideal of house unity appear frequently in surviving documents. It is clear that the primacy of the individual triumphed in the late 1960s, a development not unique to Eclectic. The cultural revolution of that decade changed the Fraternity, Wesleyan, and indeed the country, forever. The Vietnam War and the increasing opposition to it among the general population, but especially among young people, led to a growing lack of respect for authority and traditions. "Turn on, tune in, drop out" became the mantra for a generation. It was not a healthy prescription for an organization that depended on a fair degree of disciplined commitment and participation. The reduction in the weekly scope of literary exercises in November 1960 was an early sign of the coming wave, and the increasing number of brothers who failed to attend the weekly meetings was a clear indication of reduced willingness to observe the Fraternity's traditional norms of behavior. Ignoring provisions of the Eclectic Constitution at an accelerating pace was another sign of the breakdown of respect for tradition, a key element of fraternity life in the old sense.

Boorish and even destructive behavior became more and more common in the House as the decade of the 1960s advanced. Much of this was probably associated with increasing use of alcohol and illicit drugs by many brothers. Such behavior and the refusal to acknowledge financial obligations to the eating club, the Fraternity and the Socratic Literary Society, which had made a number of loans to undergraduates that were not repaid, drove a further wedge between undergraduates and alumni. The Socratic Literary Society continued to try to work with and encourage the undergraduates, but by the end of the 1970s it virtually ceased to function. Fewer and fewer alumni contributed after donations were no longer tax deductible, and many alumni felt alienated from the House, which no longer resembled the institution they knew as undergraduates.

The exclusiveness inherent in the fraternities was no longer acceptable to many. Shibboleths composed in the nineteenth century such as the high-flown rhetoric (some in Latin) of the initiation ceremony; the Greek motto "Phusis (nature), Nus (mind), Theios (God)"; and the references in fraternity songs to "precepts spun from honor, truth, and right," "a temple grander, lovelier than the world has ever known," and "our mystic union" increasingly did not ring true in questioning and perhaps cynical ears. The purpose of the Fraternity as expressed in the Constitution and initiation ceremony no longer spoke to members:

> The object of this society shall be the establishment of a fraternal league for the mutual improvement of its members in all the virtues of scholarly, literary, and manly character. . . . We aim to be scholars, but our connection is not exclusively literary. It is social also and moral. We wish to link together a band of literary friends in whose midst, while the head is improved, the heart shall not be forgotten.[10]

The University increasingly took over the role played in earlier days by the fraternities, that of feeding, housing, providing venues for socializing, and offering a broad range of course offerings that would satisfy the most diverse tastes. The fraternities, including Eclectic, no longer occupied a crucial niche in Wesleyan life. Arthur E. Sutherland Jr. (1923)

recognized this as early as 1961, when in contributing to the SLS he urged his fellow Socrats to consider gifting the House to the University for use as a Harvard house-type organization. (He taught law at Harvard and was a member of a multigenerational Eclectic family.)[11] Lastly, the reinstitution of coeducation in 1968–69 may well have contributed to the demise of the old Eclectic, although exactly how is hard to say. (Women were admitted to the "new" Eclectic in the early 1970s.)

Was the demise of the old institution inevitable? Without a national headquarters to provide support and, most critically, without a financial "angel" (or angels) to bankroll the old Eclectic, the answer, alas, is probably yes. Alpha Delta Phi, also a fraternity with a literary tradition, survived with many traditions intact. They had several alumni of considerable means who came to their rescue financially and morally. These alumni carried Alpha Delt financially as long as necessary and helped solve the problem of integration of women into the local chapter, while preserving the ties with the unintegrated chapters elsewhere. If Eclectic had been fortunate enough to have had such alumni, it might have imitated Alpha Delta Phi. That can only remain a matter of speculation, however.

For those of us who remember the old Eclectic, we have our memories. If this book helps stir those memories, perhaps the words of the last stanza of Stephen Henry Olin's "Tela Mystica" still apply:

So may we live that when our lives shall end,
Some mem'ry of us with that web may blend,
And still some strength or beauty to it lend.
So may we die.

View of the interior of the house at 200 High Street: the library with portraits of Billy Rice and Judge Reynolds on the left (north) wall.

*View of the interior of the house: the parlor with a grand piano.
The atmosphere was like that of a New York club.*

John M. Van Vleck (1850). One of three giants of Eclectic in the late nineteenth and early twentieth centuries. Often referred to as "Uncle Johnny," he was a professor at Wesleyan for more than fifty years and served as acting president three times.

William N. "Billy" Rice (1865). Another of the giants, he was called "the greatest Eclectic" and strongly influenced the Fraternity for a hundred years. He also served as acting president of the University 1907–9.

Stephen H. Olin (1866). Author of "Tela Mystica," the anthem of the Fraternity. He and his wife made significant contributions to the decor of the house. He served as acting president of the University 1922–23.

Incorporating the Socratic Literary Society of Middletown.

Resolved by this Assembly, SEC. 1.   That John M. Van Vleek, George G. Reynolds, Gilbert Haven, William Rice, Stephen H. Olin, R. B. Gwillim, their associates and successors, be, and they hereby are, ordained, constituted, and appointed a body politic and corporate, by the name of the Socratic Literary Society, and by that name they shall be capable of sueing and being sued, pleading and being impleaded ; may have a common seal, and alter the same at pleasure ; may purchase, receive, hold, and convey any estate, real or personal, not exceeding fifteen thousand dollars, and may establish such by-laws and regulations as may be necessary or convenient, not inconsistent with the laws of this state.

SEC. 2.   This act may be altered, amended or repealed at the pleasure of the general assembly.

Approved, July 5th, 1870.

Original Socratic Literary Society Charter of 1870. It formally established the alumni organization under the laws of Connecticut and permitted it to own property, leading to the construction of the first Eclectic house in 1882.

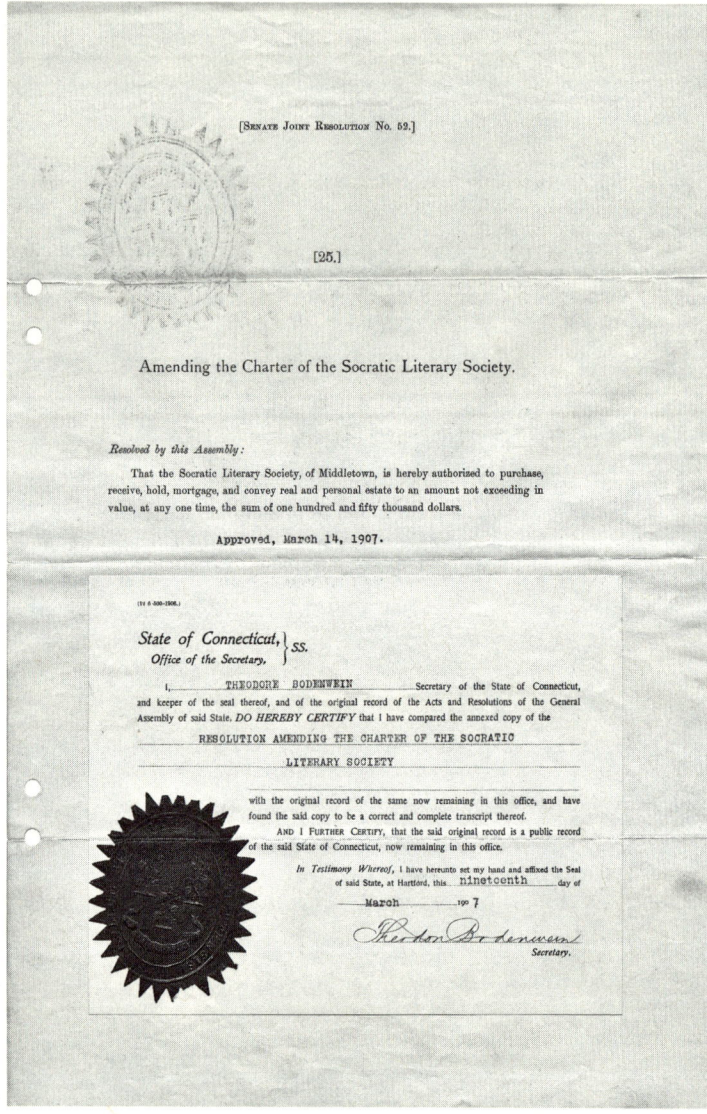

[Senate Joint Resolution No. 52.]

[25.]

Amending the Charter of the Socratic Literary Society.

Resolved by this Assembly:

That the Socratic Literary Society, of Middletown, is hereby authorised to purchase, receive, hold, mortgage, and convey real and personal estate to an amount not exceeding in value, at any one time, the sum of one hundred and fifty thousand dollars.

Approved, March 14, 1907.

[tf 6-500-1906.]

State of Connecticut, } ss.
Office of the Secretary,

I, THEODORE BODENWEIN Secretary of the State of Connecticut, and keeper of the seal thereof, and of the original record of the Acts and Resolutions of the General Assembly of said State, **DO HEREBY CERTIFY** that I have compared the annexed copy of the RESOLUTION AMENDING THE CHARTER OF THE SOCRATIC LITERARY SOCIETY

with the original record of the same now remaining in this office, and have found the said copy to be a correct and complete transcript thereof.

AND I FURTHER CERTIFY, that the said original record is a public record of the said State of Connecticut, now remaining in this office.

In Testimony Whereof, I have hereunto set my hand and affixed the Seal of said State, at Hartford, this nineteenth day of

March 190 7

Theodore Bodenwein
Secretary.

The 1907 Amendment to the SLS Charter. It increased the allowed holdings of the alumni organization from $15,000 to $150,000 to permit the new house at 200 High Street.

Burton H. Camp (1901). Prominent Eclectic of the first half of the twentieth century. He was professor of mathematics for more than forty years and was the unofficial "Grand Old Man" of Eclectic from the 1940s until his death at age ninety-nine in 1980.

Howard B. Matthews (1928). Also prominent in Wesleyan and fraternity affairs. He served as vice president and treasurer of the University (1950–69). His reminiscences on fraternity life in the 1920s (quoted in chapter 10) are most enlightening.

John W. Macy Jr. (1938). He probably occupied the highest position in the U.S. government of any Eclectic as chairman of the Civil Service Commission (1961–69) and in other positions. He also served as executive vice president of the University (1958–61).

Typical Eclectics of the mid-1950s.
The picture includes the Delegations of 1956 through 1959.
The author is third from the left in the second to bottom row.

Erich Fichtner, "The Chief."
Here, he dances with Miss Peggy
J. Emerich, the future wife of
William E. G. "Weg" Thomas
(1959).

Fall house party, 1956.
"While the head is improved, the heart shall not be forgotten."

SIX SELECTED "SONGS OF PHI NU THETA"

Note: The songs are copied from *Songs of Phi Nu Theta — The Eclectic Society*, published in 1931 for the Centenary of Wesleyan University by the Socratic Literary Society. They are the songs that were still sung in the 1950s.

Phi Nu Theta Floreat.

Air in 2d Tenor

WM. NORTH RICE, '65.

GAUDEAMUS IGITU

1. Phi Nu The - ta flo - re - at, Vi - vat in ae - ter-num
2. Per - lus - tra - mus amplumor - bem Du - ce Phi Nu The - ta;
3. Con - for - ma - mus an - i - mum; E - a - dem ma - gis - tra,
4. Al - ti - or - a dis - ci - mus, De - um ad - o - ra - re;
5. Prae-di - ca - mus ig - i - tur, Lu - men te su - per-num

Dum se - nes - cit lu - naet cres - cit At-que sol qui non lan-gue-scit
Car - mi - na sphe-rar*um* au - di - mus Reg - u - las na - tu-rae sci-mus
A - lit men-tem co - gi - ta - tis; Bo - nis, ve - ris, al - tis, gra-tis,
Op - ti - mam sci - en - ti - am, Ve-ram sa - pi - en-ti - am,
Al - ta su - per glo - ri - as, Ae-mu - la - rum flo-re - as,

Curr*um* a - git di - ur - num, Curr*um* a - git di - ur-num
Op - e - ra con - su - e - ta, Op - e - ra con - su - e - ta.
E - ji - cit sin - is - tra, E - ji - cit sin - is - tra
Et fra - tres a - ma - re, Et fra - tres a - ma - re.
Vi - vas in ae - ter - num, Vi - vas in ae - ter - num

With Joyful Songs We Come.

MORRIS B. CRAWFORD '74

PATRIOTIC GLEE

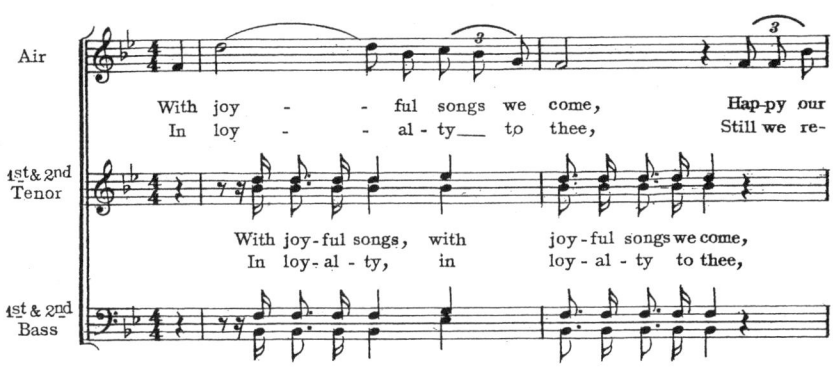

Air

With joy - - ful songs we come, Hap-py our
In loy - - al - ty___ to thee, Still we re-

1st & 2nd
Tenor

With joy-ful songs, with joy-ful songs we come,
In loy-al - ty, in loy - al - ty to thee,

1st & 2nd
Bass

hearts, Hap-py and gay, Our old ___ Ec-lec-tic
joice, Still we re - joice, Our old ___ Fra-ter-ni-

Hap-py our hearts, Hap-py and gay, Our old, our
Still we re-joice, Still we re-joice, Our old, our

3   *rit.*   *3*   Fin

home,   Tri - bute of   love fond - ly   to thee   we   pay.
ty,   Glad - ly thy   sons   ev - er   o - bey   thy   voice.

old   Ec - lec - tic home, Tri - bute of   love fond - ly   to thee   we   pay.
old   Fra - ter - ni - ty, Glad - ly thy   sons   ev - er   o - bey   thy   voice.

Air in 2d Tenor

Mem - 'ries of   the gol - den   days of yore When   loy - al - ty   to thee   we
Hopes of hon - or   in   the   fu - ture bright, Grow   bright - er while   to thee   our

vowed for - ev - er   more,   Come   bright - ly   waft - ing o'er   the
feal - ty here we plight;   No   fears   their   mourn - ful shad - ows

D.C. al Fin

van - ished years To   chase   a - way   our   care   and   fears.
o'er   us   fling; While   Phi   Nu The - ta's praise   we   sing.

The Shrine of Phi Nu Theta.

STEPHEN H. OLIN, '66.

Battle Hymn of the Republic.

1. There's a tem-ple gran-der, love-lier than the
2. In the wor-ship of this tem-ple, love and
3. A con-se-cra-ted broth-er-hood a-
4. Thy glo-ries in the past, — thy —

world has ev-er known, 'Tis the shrine of Phi Nu The-ta, in its
joy and rev-'rence blend, To the Good, the True, the Beau-ti-ful, rise
round the al-tar stand, With— ear-nest minds, u-ni-ted hearts, and
eld-er sons can tell; Thy— glo-ries in the pre-sent, our—

mys-tic state a-lone; Less-er lights ap-pear in sys-tems; on-ly
prais-es with-out end; While in-es-ti-ma-ble bless-ings on the
hand linked fast in hand, With hon-or bright and pur-pose high, a
ar-dent love com-pel; The cho-rus of the fu-ture in thy

one   sun   ev - er   shone;   The   "cho - sen"   are   but   few.
wor - ship - pers   de - scend   From   Phi   Nu   The - ta   dear.
true   Ec - lec - tic   band,   They   Phi   Nu   The - ta   serve.
praise shall   ev - er   swell,   O   Phi   Nu   The - ta   dear.

CHORUS. Air in 1st Bass.

1st & 2d Tenor.

Glo - ry be to Phi Nu The - ta, Loved and hon-ored Phi Nu The - ta; Th

1st & 2d Bass.

worth - y praise of Phi Nu The - ta, Ec - lec - tic broth - ers sing!

Eclectic Shone!

Words by
JOHN A. PATTEN, '21.

Music by
RUSSELL MACINNES, '23

1. When Psi U still wore ba-by clothes; be-fore Chi Psi was known, Ec-lec-tic shone!___ Ec-lec-tic shone! (BANG! BANG!) When D K E was still un-born and Al-pha Delt un-known, Ec-lec-tic shone!___ Ec-lec-tic shone! (BANG! BANG!)

2. Oh Eve she wore a sis-ter pin which made her A-dam's own, Ec-lec-tic shone!___ Ec-lec-tic shone! (BANG! BANG!) But Cain al-though a leg-a-cy was pledged Psi Up-si-lon, Ec-lec-tic shone!___ Ec-lec-tic shone! (BANG! BANG!)

We'll sing the praise of Phi Nu The-ta dear and of the gol-den scroll so

We'll sing the praise of Phi Nu The-ta dear ___ and of the gol-den scroll so

We'll sing the praise of Phi Nu, Phi Nu The-ta dear and of the gol-den scroll so

Praise ___ of Phi Nu The-ta dear and of the gol-den scroll so

bright ___ Her sons shall ral-ly round from far and near and for Ec-lec - tic

bright ___ Her sons shall ral-ly round from far and near and for Ec-lec-tic they wil

bright, the gol-den scroll, Her sons shall ral-ly round from far and near and for Ec-lec-tic they wil

bright ___ Her sons shall ral-ly round from far and near and for Ec-lec - tic

they will fight!   We'll give her all   our strength and ev-en more, and we will

fight!____   We'll give her all   our   strength and ev - en more, ___ and we will

they will fight! We'll give her all   our   strength and ev - en, ev-en more, and we will

they will fight!   all _____ our strength and ev-en more, and we will

serve her to the end: ___ So give a cheer and all ac-claim the name of   Phi Nu The-ta!

serve her to the end: ___ So give a cheer and all ac-claim the name of   Phi Nu The-ta!

serve her to the end: ___ So give a cheer and all ac-claim the name of   Phi Nu The-ta!

serve her to the end: ___ So give a cheer and all ac-claim the name of   Phi Nu The-ta!

Initiation Song.

Air in 2d Tenor

C. L. RICE

"Autum

Greet-ing from our mys - tic un - ion To her last a - dop - ted
Each for ev - 'ry oth - er car - ing, Learns his broth - er's good to
And with stern - er ef - fort. striv - ing For the Right, the True, the

sons! To her in - ner - most com - mun - ion Wel - com
prize: And with each his hon - or shar - ing, Ev - 'ry
Good. Each a bright ex - am - ple leav - ing, Shall a

we her *cho - sen* ones! To a sphere where love's the
hon - or mul - ti - plies. While in one pur - suit u
dorn the broth - er - hood. All that's no - ble, Phi Nu

cen - ter, Round which hate — and en - vy cease; — Where dis
nit - ed, Cul - ture of the un-meas-ured mind, — Each to
The - ta Bids her vo - ta - ries re - vere. —— Fra - tres,

sen - sions nev - er en - ter, To a fel - low-ship of peace.
brav - er toil in - cit - ed, Shall a rich - er har - vest bind.
So - ci - i, Sal - ve - te! You are count - ed worth - y here.

Tela Mystica.

Air in 2d Tenor.

EPHEN H. OLIN, '66.   INTEGER VITAE

1. She stands and weaves the hang - ings of her shrine, The var - ied threads in one com - plete de - sign, Her fly - ing fin - gers tire - less - ly en - twine, That God - dess fair.

2. A - cross the loom in lev - el lines of light, Are stretched the woof threads, ev - en, strong and bright. Her pre - cepts, spun from hon - or, truth and right, Shine fade - less there.

3. She weaves a mys - tic, mag - ic web; for lo! Be - hind the fly - ing shut - tle, to and fro. A hun - dred cho - sen life threads swift - ly go. Thrice hap - py they!

4. All bright at first; some ev - er bright - er there, Keep - ing fair prom - ise with a - chieve - ment fair. Some soiled with sin and worn with toil and care, But loved al way.

5. For each a place her lov - ing art pro - vides, The dark - er shade with bright - er lines di - vides; The knot - ted threads be - neath the fab - ric hides From hos - tile eye.

6. So may we live that when our lives shall end, Some mem - 'ry of us with that web may blend, And still some strength or beau - ty to it lend. So may we die.

FOUNDERS' PRIZE LAUREATES

The year 1922 witnessed the establishment of the Founders' Prize. The prize was to be awarded at each Annual Meeting to two (sometimes more) members of either the junior or sophomore classes who according to active members (i.e., undergraduates) "most faithfully and effectively encouraged others in the maintenance of Eclectic traditions and ideals of character." The prize was established by Nelson C. Hubbard (1892), son of the recently deceased William P. Hubbard (1863) and grandson of Chester D. Hubbard (1840). Brother Nelson Hubbard presented the first prizes to John A. Dunn (1923) and Edward G. Budd (1923) at the 1922 Annual Meeting. In the late 1940s, the Prize began to be awarded mostly to seniors. Awardees include:

1922 John A. Dunn (1923) and Edward G. Budd (1923)

1923 Lawrence B. Hillyer (1924), Charles M. Lester (1924), and Theodore C. Lyman (1925)

1924 Theodore C. Lyman (1925), Leonard B. Beach (1925), and Robert M. Boyd (1926)

1925 Roland W. Hess (1926) and Edward M. Thorndike (1926)

1926 Ralph F. Bischoff (1927) and Henry C. Kuhl (1927)

1927 Rosswell H. Douglass (1928) and Howard B. Matthews (1928)

1928 William E. Jackson Jr. (1929) and Edwin G. Schneider (1929)

1929 James F. Bagg (1930) and William W. Bailey (1931)

1930 John A. Kouwenhoven (1931) and Robert F. Beach (1932)

1931 Robert F. Beach (1932) and Henry G. Ingraham (1933)

1932

1933 Raymond M. Mitchell (1933) and Henry G. Ingraham (1933)

1934 Bernard H. White (1935) and Keith G. Huntress (1935)

1935 W. Waldo Beach (1937) and John B. Roxby (1936)

1936 W. Waldo Beach (1937) and Raymond J. Walsh (1937)

1937 Raymond J. Walsh (1937) and Richard W. Petherbridge (1938)

1938 James E. McCabe (1939) and Robert M. Stevenson (1939)

1939 William B. Whiting (1940) and Wendell B. Coote (1940)

1940 Wallace B. Hussong (1941) and John N. Moore (1941)

1941 Robert R. Marsh (1942) and Richard E. Hickey (1943)

1942   Richard E. Hickey (1943) and William H. Satterthwaite III
       (1943)
1943   Willets H. Shotwell Jr. (1944) and Roger C. Voter (1944)
1944   Mark Barlow Jr. (1946) and Robert H. McManus (1946)
1945   Malcom A. Bagshaw (1946) and Seward R. Coffin (1946)
1946
1947
1948
1949   Frank H. Wenner (1949) and Alexander B. Porter (1949)
1950
1951   F. Kingston Berlew (1951) and William A. Hunt (1951)
1952   David R. Daniel (1952) and Nathan T. Griscom (1952)
1953   Atwood P. Dunham (1953) and David B. Jenkins (1953)
1954   Benjamin F. Cope (1954) and William R. Bailey (1954)
1955   Charles F. Smith (1955) and L. Lee Allison (1955)
1956   Somerville Parker (1956) and Allen H. Haas (1956)
1957   Edward C. Porter (1957) and C. David Spencer (1957)
1958   T. Ramsey Thorp (1958) and Donald M. Hill III (1958)
1959   John A. H. Briscoe (1959) and William B. B. Moody (1959)
1960
1961
1962
1963
1964
1965
1966   Gary B. Conger (1966) and Joel B. Russ (1966)
1967
1968
1969

Although mention of the Founders' Prize is made in available records through the late 1960s, names are lacking for a number of years,
as indicated by the blanks.

MARTIN PRIZE LAUREATES

William W. Martin (1874) offered a bequest to the Socratic Literary Society to establish a Martin Prize, which was accepted by the Annual Meeting of the Socrats of June 17, 1932. The prize, the interest income from the bequest of $1,000, was to be awarded annually to the freshman with the highest record of achievement at midyear. The recipient each year would be obligated to read several historical documents relating to the Fraternity, including an address of the donor. According to the terms of the bequest, the corpus would revert with no restrictions to the general funds of the Socratic Literary Society twenty-one years after the death of the last member of the delegations of 1928 through 1932. In 1938, all reading obligations connected with the Martin Prize were canceled at the request of the donor and by action of the House.

1932	Clarence K. Aldrich (1935) and Horace K. Burr (1935)
1933	Blake G. Reynolds (1936)
1934	William E. Manring (1937)
1935	Arnold W. McClure (1938) and David N. Kendall (1938)
1936	
1937	Eliot D. Allen (1940)
1938	Wallace B. Hussong (1941)
1939	Raymond R. Marsh (1942)
1940	Richard E. Hickey (1943)
1941	Scott M. Heaton (1944)
1942	Paul D. Tillett Jr. (1945)
1943	Robert Henry McManus (1946)
1944	Arthur R. Clemett (1946)
1945	
1946	Mark B. Holzman (1949)
1947	Peter J. Fernald (1950)
1948	John G. Reynolds (1951)
1949	Nathan T. Griscom (1952)
1950	David B. Jenkins (1953)
1951	Harvey A. Lerner (1954)
1952	Norman A. Clemens (1955)

1953 Somerville Parker (1956)
1954 Mark B. Feldman (1957)
1955 *John H. Hobbs (1958)
1956 Richard M. Wenner (1959)
1957 Robert A. Mortimer (1960)
1958 *Joseph A. Powers (1961)
1959 Gary R. Wanerka (1962)

* Presumed because of tradition, but not confirmed in records

Note: No records of the awarding of the Martin Prize exist in available records after 1959. The funds were identified in correspondence as late as the mid-1970s, but laureates were not mentioned.

RICE PRIZE LAUREATES

The annual Rice Prize was established by vote of the Regular Meeting of May 18, 1954, in memory of Horace B. Rice (1954n), who had died the previous year. The criteria for selection by the senior delegation was that member of the junior delegation who had demonstrated the most personal progress during his years in Eclectic.

1954   Robert M. Burrer (1955)
1955   Allen H. Haas (1956)
1956   Mark B. Feldman (1957)
1957
1958   Robert C. Chase (1959)
1959   Bruce M. Dow (1960)

No records mention the awarding of the prize after 1959.

LIST OF MATRONS

The following lists those individuals who are mentioned in the formal documents of the Eclectic Society or the Socratic Literary Society as serving as matrons.

Name	Years (Estimate)
Miss Susie E. Clark[1]	1902–19
Miss Waldron	1919–20
Miss Farnsworth	1920–27
Mrs. Thorpe[2]	1927 (half year)
Mrs. Boynton	1928–30
Mrs. West	1930–38

Beginning in 1938–39 Erich "The Chief" and Kaethe Fichtner served as food service concessionaires, living in the House and effectively functioning as house "parents." Upon Erich Fichtner's retirement in June 1962 a number of different arrangements for food service were tried. The last name mentioned in the records of a person occupying such a position was Ray Hoagland (Minutes of April 6, 1966), who was still involved with the House in the early 1970s.

PROFESSOR BURTON H. CAMP'S ADDRESS, "BILLY RICE"

When the undergraduates asked me to say a few words about some older Eclectics at one of their meetings, I chose to speak of Billy Rice, and reflected with shock that Billy was further away from them than the founders had been from me. This is a repetition of some of the things I said then. It is by no means an adequate essay on William North Rice, but it is high time that things about him should be in print, and I hope that more will come later from others more able than I to write about him.

First of all I am talking about him as a real person, not as a little god. Brother F. M. Davenport said at a recent Initiation that he was our "greatest Eclectic," and I shall say so too presently, but I am not going to describe him as a superman. This for two reasons. First I married into the family. I married his niece. Now I hope the girl you marry will be a super woman, but it is too much to ask that in-laws shall be more than human also. Secondly, I was for a long time a colleague of Billy's, and so far as I know no member of any faculty thinks of any other member, no matter how superior, as without some human faults. Minor faults, no doubt, but in all candor there they are. I make no apology for adopting this attitude, for after all it was as a real person that Billy dwelt among us.

The statement that he was our greatest Eclectic does not mean even that he was the greatest man among all who had been Eclectics, although of course he would be a strong candidate for that distinction. It refers both to his intrinsic greatness and also to his long and important association with the undergraduate Eclectic fraternity. He graduated in '65, as the Civil War ended, went to Yale to get a Ph.D. in geology, and then returned to teach for fifty years at Wesleyan. During all that half century he was very close to the undergraduate fraternity and dominated the Socrats.

As a member of the faculty he was in the forefront of everything that happened and served as acting president part of the time. At first he taught many things. He used to say he had a bench, not a chair. Eventually, and in my time, he taught only geology and a great course in

Science and Religion. He was highly regarded as a geologist and was honored by his national society. He traveled far and wide on geological trips, in Europe, in the far west, and in Alaska, all at his own expense, for the college financed nothing of that sort in those days. He did not, however, make distinguished contributions to geology such as might have been expected of a scientist of his genius. The reason was that he gave himself without stint to the college, to his students, to city and to church. He was always on hand when anything was stirring in any of these places, and usually when it was not. He said (quoting somebody else) that a suitable epitaph for him would be: "Here lies a man who might have done something if he had not done something else."

But the something else was important. I refer especially to his greatest course, "Science and Religion," that began in the days when not to believe in Genesis was like being a fellow traveler now. Boys came to college brought up in the tradition of inerrant Scripture. They were destined to lose that anyhow, Billy or no Billy. (I lost mine in high school.) But Billy did help the process with great vigor. He not only denied Genesis in the Old Testament. He denied all the miracles in the New Testament, except one: he believed in the Resurrection, and gave us what were then strong reasons for that belief. This course was a forerunner to the humanities courses given now in that it embraced all sorts of knowledge, science, philosophy, history, and of course Biblical literature. It had an advantage over the humanities in that it was not required and had a unifying principle—the problem of how to think about religious matters in an age of science—and this of necessity involved a consideration of all these other matters. In this course Billy went through for us the travail of his own soul, an honest soul who would not deceive himself and could not deceive others, brought up in one tradition to which he was emotionally attached, but necessarily faced with denial after denial of things he had been taught to believe sacred. He was eloquent in this course. Many of us were stirred deeply by these religious storms, but we were not utterly lost, and we would have been had it not been for him. We had to throw overboard a lot that we had treasured, but we did keep our sanity. And so we were grateful that he decided not to become a distinguished geologist.

He was a man of very small stature, but of great physical health and endurance. He told me once that he usually went to bed about midnight and got up at about six, regularly, sleeping perfectly from the moment his head touched the pillow until something told him it was now time to get up and read his Greek Testament. Then he prayed (aloud), went down stairs to a leisurely breakfast, and then to work. Everything he did he did painstakingly, even to the keeping of his cash account. I remember one entry, written with a penmanship that an engraver might envy, "Hoop for Eddie, 50 cents." He was a modest man, but he did not prate of his modesty. He looked upon himself objectively. My wife asked him once if he had been an infant prodigy. "Why no," he replied, "I didn't even read until I was three!" They say that when a small child he found an old arithmetic book around the house, and went to his mother with it and asked her how to do one of the problems in the last part of the book. She replied that she could not make him understand that one until he had understood those that came before, and had he done all the preceding problems. "No," he said, "I have done one or two in each set of problems. It would be silly to do them all." He had a wonderful memory, a love of literary things, and an excellent sense of humor, this last of a limited and strictly high grade variety—nothing raucous was included. Anything of the rough and tumble variety not only did not seem funny to him, he simply could not understand how anybody else could think it funny. He was of course a righteous man. Somehow sin never seemed to tempt him. I used to compare him with Winchester. Winchester was a good man too. He did not sin either, but Winchester wanted to, and Billy didn't. The most important thing about Billy's character was, I think, his devotion to the truth, which he sought as a pearl of great price, and unlike some other honest people it did not occur to him to brag about his honesty. It was quite simply a natural part of him. Once, during his last years, we talked of an important matter which he had discussed in the book he had written summarizing that course. It was a very important matter, and he stated that his recent reading had led him to believe that he had been in error. "That (said he) changes a lot of my conclusions," and then he added that he would like to reconsider the matter and write the book over. There he was at that age ready to reconsider all that he had fought for so long. This was scientific integrity at its maximum; and I could only look at him in silent wonder. I knew he would never rewrite the book, but I knew I would tell that story, when I had the chance.

I spoke of his memory. Once in our home the conversation fell on "Horatius at the Bridge," and we asked him if he could remember who had stood on the right and who on the left. Enjoying the quickness of his response I then put this one to him: "What is the sine of 60 degrees?" He gave the wrong answer at first and I chided him with it. Then he thought for a moment and said, "No, of course not. It is the square root of three over two." I asked him how remembered that after all these sixty-odd years. "I don't remember it (he said), I work it out."

Our greatest Eclectic. For half a century and more he was with us, and intimately. He praised us when we did well, and, he prayed over us when we did ill, and there were few of our secrets that he didn't know (there were a few). This was because he worked so hard for the fraternity and had to be close to it. On almost all occasions which I can remember he was the final speaker at our banquets, and he was always wanted. There was, of course, an occasional scoffer, and some said he was repetitious. In a sense he was that. He did not repeat the words, but he did repeat the idea, and this was the idea that he repeated so often, his own faith in the spiritual worth of the fraternity. To him it was more than a fraternity, and he loved it deeply, and well he might. He and Olin together had in their undergraduate days written our Initiation service in its present form; they and his mother and his brothers and his son had written many of our songs, and his speeches and those songs all said the same thing: this is what we were here for, to live nobly. I can still hear him say it. "All that's noble," his mother wrote, "Phi Nu Theta bids her votaries revere," and we sing it at every Initiation. He did say this over and over again, and of those who listened, some believed, and to those who believed he gave of his spirit, and they made his words come true. So it now happens that strangers say to me, members of our faculty who may have never heard of him, and who don't think highly of fraternities anyhow, "Eclectic does seem to have something about it that is different." They do not know why, and there are many reasons, but if you had to say it in two words those words would have to be: Billy Rice.

Delivered at the Annual Meeting Banquet
June 1952

PROFESSOR BURTON H. CAMP'S ADDRESS, "UNCLE JOHNNY"

Brother Eclectics:

I have been asked to write out what I said at our banquet in June. Those remarks do not seem to me to be specially suited to written discourse, but for what they may be worth here they are.

Since writing that paper about Billy Rice I have been thinking of another great Eclectic who was also a Wesleyan professor, J. M. VanVleck, Uncle Johnny we called him. Billy Rice used to say that Wesleyan University owed more to him than to any other man. Perhaps Billy was over modest at this point. He was referring to incidents that happened before my time, and I would not know, but he said it on more than one occasion, and evidently felt quite certain of it. I am not going to indulge in extensive reminiscences of Uncle Johnny. I only want to tell you one way in which he influenced me. If I can tell you that adequately, then he will have come here tonight and said something to you also.

First of all some things he did not do. Uncle Johnny was a professor of mathematics and astronomy, but he made no significant contribution to either of these sciences. He might well have. He had the mental powers and the energy to do distinguished work. As many of you know his grandson is now a distinguished mathematical physicist at Harvard. But as in the case of most men of that time, the college demanded too much other work of him to permit time for research. Also, when I knew him he was not by modern standards a particularly good teacher. (Here I described briefly one of his classes.) But his character shone through his teaching. He thought he was teaching us astronomy, but he wasn't, or if he was, we quickly forgot it. But, without knowing it, he was teaching us something else which we would never forget.

It would be too little to say that Uncle Johnny was an honest man, and that he had scientific integrity. What I have in mind now is more subtle than that. He had one of the cleanest minds I ever knew, and by clean I do not mean now the opposite of smutty. If a matter should be arrived at rationally, Uncle Johnny would not stoop to make an emotional appeal instead. If an action could be explained in several ways, he would not dissemble by giving other than the primary reasons, and if you asked him a question he would answer that question, not some other. The reason for all this, we felt, was that all his life he had not hesitated to ask himself the right questions, and had not side-stepped the answers.

To illustrate. When I was a boy there was a band of men who called themselves Kickapoo Indians. They traveled apparently like gypsies, and would park their covered wagon in a vacant lot at night. Attracting a crowd by flares they would put on a show as follows. First a brave would come out and display his strength and vigor in various ways. "See how strong we are." Then another would come out and describe dreadful diseases which we were all likely to get, and then he would put on the table a bottle of Kickapoo Indian Sagwa — 25 cents. No other argument, but many takers. Not many years ago a distinguished orator came to the Wesleyan Chapel. He began by describing certain thrilling incidents in all of which he happened to be the hero. Then he described the horrors of World War III which was certain to come unless we bought his pre-scription which he then laid on the table. No other argument, but the applause was long and loud. Uncle Johnny would not have done this. Either he got you clean or not at all. Incidentally, he almost certainly would not have applauded either, for he did have an obstinate streak.

Many years ago, as I sat in my study at home, my little daughter came running to me, and asked me why was I doing some thing or other. I replied: "Well, for one reason" — and then gave her a perfectly honest answer. She looked at me for a moment, as a child will, and then said: "What's the other reason, Daddy?" I have a feeling that Uncle Johnny would have given the other reason first. My third illustration has to do with a friend of mine, Fred ____, who went to Dartmouth. Fred was a charming youth. He played on the hockey team, and the boys all liked him, and he could get anything he wanted from anybody just by ask-ing for it. But he did have a little trouble with his grades. So he chose a certain course in art and he chose it wisely. Since then he has been in business, and I imagine that what he learned in college helped him in business. If you wish to make an investment, and do not wish to specu-late, you consider the dividend record of the security. Did it skip one for example in the depression? Fred considered the record of this course, and it was perfect. Nobody in its long history had ever flunked. So he took it, and all went well until Midyears. Then when he saw the paper he thought at first he had got hold of the wrong one, but no that was not it. So he went to the professor and said that perhaps those matters had been taken up while he was away on the hockey team—which, as the professor would remember had had some victories, and that he knew a good deal about the course, but that somehow or other those particular questions—"Fred," said the kindly old man, "Go back to your seat and ask yourself a question and answer it." So Fred did, and all went well until June. He played hockey some more and the boys liked him some more, and in June the same thing happened again except that he couldn't find the professor. So Fred asked himself a question and answered it as before. A few days later he met the professor in the street, and the .professor looked at him sadly. "I am sorry;" said he, "if you had only asked a proper question, I would have passed you."

What Uncle Johnny seems to me to be saying to Eclectics tonight is this: "Ask yourself the proper question, and answer it. Answer that question, not some other. Do not side-step."

What is this question? It is none other than the one you undergraduates have been asking of the Faculty in the Argus this spring: What do you live by? This is now the question that the College is asking the fraternities. And why should we not ask ourselves that question, boldly? And what is the answer?

If you ask me I think: I should have to flounder around a bit, same as the Faculty did, for I only know the answer in part. But if I did know it completely I would not tell the undergraduates, for they would not take it from me, and if they would take it from me, I still would not give it, for this is the sort of thing they have to find out for themselves. But surely one can indicate the general direction which the answer will take. Consider the antecedent question: What is a college for? I do not know the complete answer, but surely it is not too much to say that it has something to do with the search for wisdom. Wisdom is a noble objective, for only by wisdom can we escape the slavery of superstition. What is a fraternity for? Surely it has something to do with the objective of the college of which it is a part.

I can put this in another way. Most of our fraternities were founded in the nineteenth century when secret societies were the fashion. That secrecy element is of no importance now. But the founders did something else than establish secret societies. They developed forms of education which the College did not provide. They formed debating societies and groups in which they read each others' literary compositions. In those days, remember, the only electives in sophomore year were a choice between Hebrew and calculus. Now it is up to the present founders—and we are always founding our fraternities anew—to do for 1953 what the first founders did for 1853, or whenever it was. I believe in a combination of education from the bottom up, if you don't mind my calling it that, as well as from the top down, democratically inspired education, not merely autocratically controlled. I have no doubt that by 1953 standards our education from the top is as far out of step with student needs as it was in 1853 by the then standards, or at any rate that sort of situation is bound to occur periodically. Now this is that part of the answer which I wouldn't know, and the undergraduates would know. Let them then think about it consciously and then put it into effect. I urge this not in order to save fraternities. Far from it. If indeed they have served their purpose, they should fade away. I say it because I think they have not served their purpose and that they may have a more satisfying life. For there is nothing so invigorating as the consciousness that one is doing something that he knows is worthwhile. Once let a fraternity—and in all this I am including the non-fraternity group also—recognize that it is a valid educational unit, in its own way but in its own right, then suddenly it is grown up. From then on it will continue to enjoy winning games from its playmates, but the important thing will be that it has a job to do in a world of affairs.

I think I have rational grounds for hope—partly from conversations with men from other fraternities and from J. Wesley Club as well as with Eclectics—that a movement of this sort actually is beginning. If it can only develop, and if ultimately every group at Wesleyan shall find that it does have something like this to live by, then Wesleyan will truly be the greatest college in this country. I hope the future historians will write as follows: "It had, of course, many causes, but the reason it developed first at Wesleyan is doubtless due to the fact that there already existed at Wesleyan an unusual fraternity, one that had maintained its educational ideals for over a century. That fraternity had the vision and led the way." So to the undergraduates then I would say this: If you will now let Uncle Johnny help you, you and he together can do more for this college than has ever been done before.

July 3, 1953

NOTES

NOTE TO "TO THE READER"

1. The reader will note that I have used a parenthesized four-digit in-dication of class year [i.e., (1910)] for Eclectics rather than the more con-ventional notation of an apostrophe and two digits [i.e., '10] for a num-ber of reasons, which I will be happy to discuss with fuming purists. At least it's better than Harvard's system and avoids confusion when one deals with the Eclectic "clans" of three or more generations.

NOTE TO CHAPTER 1

1. The name "The Eclectic Society" was used by a group of evangeli-cal Anglican clergymen and lay persons in London, England, during the period 1783–1814. Others of the evangelical persuasion, including Methodists, also joined the group—limited to thirteen—and their ex-ercises included discussion of a topic, either religious or secular, at each biweekly meeting. Although there is no direct evidence that the founders adopted the name from their British cousins, there can be little doubt that American Methodists were acquainted with the Lon-don organization, and it may have influenced the choice of a name. For further information see Web site http://jmm.aaa.net.au/articles/12769 .htm, specifically Aaron Belz, "Plotting the World's Salvation," *Chris-tianity Today International* 23.1 (Winter 2004): 40.

NOTE TO CHAPTER 2

1. The portrait was in place in 1992 but had been ripped from the wall along with its built-in frame, by May 2006. Undergraduates stated that the portrait was intact, stored away, and evidently had been torn from the wall by persons unknown because of a rumored "treasure" se-creted behind it.

NOTES TO CHAPTER 5

1. Socratic Literary Society, Records, 1871–1968, "Introductory Note."

2. The name is listed in *Songs of Phi Nu Theta* as C. L. Rice, but no person by this name is carried in fraternity or university records. The

author is undoubtedly Charles Francis Rice (1872), who lived from 1851 to 1927.

NOTE TO CHAPTER 6

1. See discussion of President Beach's unpopularity in David Potts's *Wesleyan University 1831–1910*, 96–97.

NOTES TO CHAPTER 7

1. See David Potts, *Wesleyan University, 1831–1910*, 238–42 (appendix 3: "Enrollments").

2. In voting their sentiments on the framing and substance of debates, the members generally came down in favor of what today would be called the liberal side on social and political questions.

3. William North Rice Collection, Letter from WNR (1865) to his son Edward Loranus Rice (1892), October 18, 1896.

NOTES TO CHAPTER 8

1. Minutes of May 8, 1901.

2. Minutes of October 25, 1901.

3. Socrats Annual Meeting of June 30, 1903.

4. Potts, *Wesleyan University 1831–1910*, 335n75.

5. For a fuller description of the selection of Henry Bacon as architect, see ibid., 195.

6. E-mail from David Potts to William Moody, October 10, 2005.

7. Socrats Annual Meeting of June 26, 1906.

8. Eclectic Society Minutes of November 5, 1906.

9. One of these was of Pericles, which stood inside the entrance to the House in the 1950s. It was "kidnapped" several times by the pledge delegations of other houses, although returned more or less intact until it disappeared in the late 1960s.

10. The portrait still hung there behind its glass protective plate in 1992, one of the few relics to survive the changes of the late 1960s and subsequent events. It had been ripped from its place by May 2006, although supposedly preserved somewhere.

11. Socratic Literary Society Annual Meeting Minutes of June 25, 1907.

12. Letter from Morris B. Crawford to Eric M. North, December 12,

1936, with enclosure, Paul North Rice Papers, Eclectic Collection, Olin Library.

13. Minutes of November 24, 1899.

14. Minutes of March 7, 1900.

15. Potts, *Wesleyan University 1831–1910*, 214–15.

16. "Eclectic Frolics and Customs," memorandum to Eric M. North from Noel E. Bensinger (undated, but from the 1930s).

17. Dave Potts commented in an e-mail of October 7, 2005, on the custom at Wesleyan: "Finger-snapping applause seems to have begun in the late nineteenth century. The *Argus* for 2 May 1940 says it started at Psi U, probably in the 1870s, and was employed campus-wide by the 1890s. The *Argus* for 19 May 1913 notes finger-snapping during chapel services at the conclusion of an unusually good sermon. I have not witnessed or heard of its use by current undergraduates."

18. Minutes of December 20, 1904.

19. Minutes of January 28, 1905.

20. Minutes of March 29, 1906.

21. Minutes of March 13, 1908.

NOTES TO CHAPTER 9

1. Minutes of October 10, 1910.

2. "Eclectic Frolics and Customs," memorandum to Eric M. North from Noel E. Bensinger (undated, but from the 1930s).

3. Minutes of November 6, 1910.

4. Minutes of November 13, 1911.

5. Minutes of March 28, 1914.

6. In reading these indications of conflict between old-line values and changing mores of the early days of the twentieth century, I thought back to an exchange with my grandmother Baker (born 1886) in the summer of my sophomore year. Grandma was a Methodist Mainer of the old school with strongly held beliefs. When she noted that I was smoking and indicated that she had heard that I was learning to drink beer at college, she remonstrated, "Oh, no, Bill. Mark my words, it's a downward spiral: first it's smoking, then drinking, then gambling, then women, then drugs. That's the way it is!"

7. Letter from William North Rice (1865) to his son Edward Loranus Rice (1892), June 25, 1913, William North Rice Papers.

8. Minutes of May 12, 1914.

9. Letter from WNR to Henry Bacon, July 1, 1914, William North Rice Papers.

10. Letter from Henry Bacon to WNR, July 11, 1914, William North Rice Papers.

11. Minutes of December 4, 1914.

12. Price, *Wesleyan's First Century*, 191–92.

13. A stone-mounted brass marker on the front lawn of 200 High Street noted this fact. The marker disappeared sometime after 1960.

14. David Potts, University historian, puts the correct number at twenty-six.

15. Minutes of October 16, 1918.

16. Minutes of December 15, 1918.

17. Minutes of November 10, 1916.

18. Minutes of April 7, 1911.

19. Minutes of January 5, 1912.

20. Minutes of October 17, 1913.

21. Minutes of November 6, 1911.

22. Minutes of May 8, 1912.

NOTES TO CHAPTER 10

1. Letter from WNR to E. L. Rice, May 16, 1921, William North Rice Papers.

2. Minutes of May 11, 1921.

3. The Jackson Cup, first awarded in 1914, was presented yearly to the fraternity with the highest academic standing. In the first six years of the Cup's existence, Eclectic won first place in 1914 and 1918; second in 1915, 1917, and 1919; and third in 1916.

4. Minutes of September 29, 1919.

5. These figures are derived from a chart in the Eclectic collection in Olin Library, devised by Paul North Rice in the mid-1930s and intended for eventual use in the North/Rice Centennial history.

6. Socrats' Annual Meeting Minutes of June 18, 1920 (B.O.D. Report).

7. Socrats' Annual Meeting Minutes of June 17, 1921 (B.O.D. Report).

8. David Potts made this point during a telephone conversation of January 17, 2006.

9. Burton H. Camp (1901), the "grand old man of Eclectic" in the 1950s, like Billy North Rice a Wesleyan professor for many years and his nephew by marriage, wrote a tribute to WNR in the early 1950s, which is reproduced as appendix F. It explains wonderfully why William North Rice had such a profound influence on Eclectic for a hundred years.

10. Minutes of October 8, 1919.

11. Minutes of September 28, 1921.

12. Socrats' Annual Meeting Minutes of June 5, 1925 (B.O.D. Report).

13. Socrats' Annual Meeting Minutes of June 18, 1926 (B.O.D. Report).

14. Minutes of December 8, 1920.

15. Minutes of March 2, 1921.

16. Minutes of March 9, 1921.

17. Minutes of April 6, 1921, and April 7, 1921.

18. Minutes of April 14, 1921.

19. Minutes of September 21, 1921.

20. Socrats' Annual Meeting Minutes of June 13, 1924 (B.O.D. Report), and Minutes of November 3, 1925.

21. Minutes of March 24, 1926.

22. Socrats' Annual Meeting Minutes of June 15, 1928 (B.O.D. Report).

23. Enclosure to a letter from E. M. Thorndike to E. M. North, August 3, 1936, Paul North Rice Papers. William George Chanter, college chaplain 1928–41, taught in the ethics and religion department 1919–41 and served as dean 1930–35.

24. Paper by H. B. Matthews entitled "Notes for the Eclectic History" (undated, but about 1936), Paul North Rice Papers.

25. Minutes of September 29, 1920.

26. Annual Meeting Minutes of June 16, 1922.

27. A listing of all recorded winners of the Founders Prize is included in appendix B.

28. Minutes of September 29, 1926.

29. Minutes of November 23, 1926.

30. Socrats' Annual Meeting Minutes of June 17, 1930 (B.O.D. Report).

1. E-mail from Dave Potts, February 1, 2006.

2. According to Dave Potts, citing the *Alumnus* of January 1943, the marker was placed on the front lawn in 1942, a fact confirmed by SLS Minutes of May 15, 1942.

3. Minutes of June 12, 1931.

4. Copies of the songs that were still sung in the 1950s are included in appendix A.

5. Minutes of October 11, 1931.

6. Minutes of May 11, 1932.

7. Socrats' Annual Meeting Minutes of June 12, 1936 (B.O.D. Report).

8. Socrats' Annual Meeting Minutes of June 16, 1933 (B.O.D. Report).

9. Minutes of November 1, 1933.

10. Socrats' Annual Meeting Minutes of June 17, 1932 (B.O.D. Report).

11. Socrats' Annual Meeting Minutes of June 16, 1933 (B.O.D. Report).

12. Minutes of October 25, 1933, the year Hitler came to power.

13. Minutes of March 23, 1938, and April 6, 1938.

14. Minutes of March 4, 1936.

15. Minutes of April 29, 1936.

16. Minutes of November 18, 1936.

17. A list of names and approximate tenures of matrons is included as appendix E.

18. Minutes of November 1, 1934.

19. Minutes of April 10, 1935.

20. Minutes of October 27, 1937.

21. Minutes of December 7, 1939.

22. Minutes of the Special Socratic Literary Society Meeting of November 13, 1936.

23. Minutes of June 2, 1937.

24. *The Scroll*, March 24, 1937, 3–4.

25. Socrats' Annual Meeting Minutes of June 15, 1934 (B.O.D. Report).

26. Socrats' Annual Meeting Minutes of June 14, 1935 (B.O.D. Report).

27. Minutes of November 5, 1930.

28. Socrats' Annual Meeting Minutes of June 18, 1937, and Special Meeting of November 5, 1937.

1. Minutes of September 27, 1939.

2. Minutes of May 29, 1940.

3. Minutes of April 24, 1940.

4. Minutes of April 23, 1941.

5. The committee evidently met with some success. I remember going through the safe in the basement of the house in about 1958 and noting a collection of fraternity keys, including one from the Beta Chapter at Ohio Wesleyan. I could find no sign of the keys in the Eclectic Collection in Olin Library during my research for this book.

6. Socrats' Annual Meeting Minutes of June 13, 1941.

7. Minutes of February 4, 1942.

8. *Alumni Record*, 1953, xiii.

9. Letter from Mark Barlow Jr. (1946) to the author, February 6, 2006.

10. Ibid.

11. Socrats' Annual Meeting Minutes of May 29, 1943.

12. Minutes of March 4, 1942.

13. Minutes of February 24, 1943.

14. Letter from Mark Barlow, May 10, 2006.

15. Minutes of March 25, 1943.

16. The book, which actually contains a constitution, minutes, and signatures of members initiated between 1848 and 1859, now forms a part of the Eclectic Collection in Olin Library.

17. Epistoleus' Report, 1943–44, vol. 80, Eclectic Repository.

18. *Alumni Record*, 1953, xiii.

19. Letter from Mark Barlow Jr. (1946) to the author, February 6, 2006.

20. Annual Meeting minutes of June 24, 1944.

21. Minutes of September 6 and 13, 1944.

22. Minutes of July 9, 1945.

23. Issues of *The Scroll* for 1946 through 1950 contain much valuable information.

24. Minutes of October 15, 1947.

25. The Constitution of the Eclectic Society, Article 2, Section 5, passed June 21, 1946.

26. *The Scroll*, 25.1 (November 1946): 1.

27. Marian Fichtner Morash, the Chief's daughter, told me in a

phone conversation of April 2006 that her father was extremely proud of his election to associate membership. He wore his fraternity key on many occasions. Marian preserved it among his effects after his death in 1970. Unfortunately, the key was stolen in a household robbery a few years later.

28. Letter from Mark Barlow Jr. (1946) to the author, February 6, 2006.

29. Author's note: If anyone knows of copies of SLS minutes or BOD Reports after 1947, I would certainly appreciate copies and will make sure they are filed safely in the Eclectic Collection of the Olin Library.

30. Minutes of October 27, 1947.

31. Minutes of September 28, 1948.

32. E-mail from Michael Fairchild of February 17, 2006.

33. E-mail from William Morrill (1952), February 22, 2006.

34. Epistoleus' Report 1949/50, vol. 86 of the *Eclectic Repository*.

35. Phone conversation with Chip Forden of February 23, 2006, with photographic backup.

36. Minutes of December 15, 1948.

37. Amendment to the Constitution, Article 10, approved June 8, 1956.

38. Minutes of January 12, 1949.

39. Minutes of April 20, 1949.

40. Phone conversation with David "Chip" Forden (1952) of February 23, 2006.

NOTES TO CHAPTER 13

1. *The Scroll* 18.2 (June 1950).

2. Minutes of October 3, 1950.

3. E-mail from David W. "Pete" Peterson, February 19, 2006.

4. E-mail from William Morrill, February 22, 2006.

5. SLS letter, November 16, 1950.

6. E-mail from William Morrill, February 22, 2006.

7. See www.wesleyan.edu/admission/diversity/fraternities (accessed 2006).

8. Minutes of November 4, 1951.

9. Minutes of January 15, 1952.

10. Minutes of February 12, 1952.

11. Minutes of May 6, 1952.

12. *Eclectic Repository*, vol. 88 (1951–92), May 20, 1952.

13. Minutes of September 23, 1952.

14. E-mail from Harvey Lerner (1954), February 16, 2006.

15. E-mail from Harvey Lerner (1954), February 16, 2006.

16. *Alumni Record*, 1953, xiii.

17. E-mail from Harvey Lerner (1954), February 15, 2006.

18. The amendment was further clarified a year later, so that an abstention counted as a negative vote, and modified two year after that to require less than one negative vote for each complete unit of twelve. In the example above, four negative votes would exclude the candidate under the revised amendment of June 8, 1956.

19. *The Scroll*, vol. 22, December 1954, 1.

20. Alumni Record, 1953, xiii–xiv.

21. Minutes of October 26, 1956.

22. Ted actually gave a special topic on German university fraternal organizations.

23. Minutes of November 6, 1956.

24. Epistoleus' Report, Eclectic Repository, vol. 94 (1957–58).

25. Meeting of November 12, 1957.

26. Minutes of February 18, 1958.

27. Minutes of February 28, 1958.

28. Minutes of March 17, 1959.

29. Minutes of May 12, 1959. The questionnaire was part of the Macy Study.

30. Exactly when is unclear. There are no records available at this writing to indicate when the first Roman Catholic and Jewish brothers joined Eclectic. From anecdotal information, it appears this occurred as early as the 1910s and almost certainly by the mid-1940s.

31. A brother from the early 1940s remembers the Chief's hurried trips out of the kitchen with a water pitcher in hand to put out smoldering cigarette butts on the roof of his canvas convertible, contributed from above by Ping-Pongers who smoked.

NOTES TO CHAPTER 14

1. Minutes of February 13, 1959.

2. *Alumni Record* (*AR*), 1962, xiv.

3. *Argus*, October 3, 1958.

4. *AR*, 1962, xv.

5. Minutes of March 17, 1959.

6. Minutes of October 13, 1959.

7. Minutes of May 10, 1960.

8. Minutes of April 12, 1960.

9. Minutes of November 16,1960.

10. *The Constitution of the Eclectic Fraternity*, Article 7.

11. The latest copy of the Constitution simply notes above the text of the amendment "Passed—February 14, 1961." There is a marginal notation after the amendment "illegal."

12. Minutes of March 15, March 21, May 9, and May 16, 1961.

13. Minutes of September 27, 1961.

14. Minutes of October 3, 1961.

15. Minutes of October 11, 1961.

16. Minutes of October 24, 1961.

17. Minutes of October 30, 1961.

18. Minutes of October 31, 1961.

19. Minutes of November 7, 1961 and Bylaws of the Eclectic Fraternity, Amendment to Article 18 and 19 passed November 7, 1961.

20. Minutes of December 5, 1961.

21. Interview with George P. Morrill (1942) on March 29, 2006.

22. Comment: Throughout the Fraternity's existence, offices were created and abolished by motions at regular meetings to meet contemporary needs (e.g., steward). Other offices, such as that of Grammateus, were listed and defined in the Constitution. Strictly speaking, any change to these latter offices would require an amendment to the Constitution, rather than a simple vote of the House. It appears no such amendment was ever offered or approved in the case of the Grammateus/vice president.

23. Minutes of January 10, 1962.

24. Minutes of February 12, 1962.

25. Minutes of January 16, 1962.

26. Minutes of March 6, 1962.

27. *AR*, 1962, xv.

28. *AR*, 1971, xiii.

29. Minutes of October 16, 1962, and *Eclectic Repository*, vol. 98.

30. Ibid.

31. Minutes of October 26, 1962.

32. Minutes of March 13, 1963.

33. Minutes of April 30, 1963.

34. Minutes of May 7, 1963.

35. *Eclectic Repository*, vol. 98, nos. 1 (1962–63) and 2 (1963–64).

36. *AR*, 1971, xiii.

37. Ibid.

38. Minutes of October 27, 1964.

39. Minutes of February 23, 1965.

40. Minutes of March 9, 1965.

41. Minutes of March 16, 1965.

42. Minutes of April 13, 1965.

43. Further identified as Ray Hoagland by Seth Kaufman (1970) in a phone conversation of May 19, 2006.

44. Minutes of April 19, 1966.

45. Minutes of May 17, 1966.

46. Minutes of October 18, 1966.

47. Brother Etherington succeeded Vic Butterfield as president of the University on July 1, 1967. The times of his tenure at Wesleyan were tempestuous, and he resigned on February 7, 1970. Allegedly one of the factors that led to his departure was an essay he had written for the Hall as an undergraduate that was not politically correct in the late 1960s and was widely circulated on the campus. I suspect that this may have been the essay. The *Eclectic Repository* volume that appears to have contained it is among the eight volumes that disappeared before the rescue mission of June 1985 that turned the *Repository* over to the Archives in Olin Library.

48. The "Annals" in the 1971 *Alumni Record* give the percentage of fraternity pledges in the freshmen class as 69 percent in 1964, 60 percent in 1965, 40 percent in 1968, and 37 percent in 1969. Of course the freshman classes were increasing in size. Total undergraduate enrollments rose from 1,149 to 1,476 during the same period. *AR*, 1971, xiv–xv.

49. Minutes of October 24, 1967.

50. My listing of all initiated Eclectics by delegation and alphabetical order (to be published separately) stops with the Delegation of 1971.

51. Minutes of April 16, 1968.

52. E-mail from Michael Fairchild, February 17, 2006.

NOTES TO EPILOGUE

1. I am greatly indebted to John A. Gettier (1956) for the gift of his files on the Socratic Literary Society during and after his tenure as an officer or on the Board of Directors of the SLS and covering the years 1968–74. The files will be donated to the Eclectic Collection in Olin Library's Special Collections/Archives upon completion of this book.

2. Letter from the chairman of the SLS Board of Directors, William C. Gordon (1955), September 17, 1970.

3. Gift and Leaseback of Socratic Literary Society Real Estate to Wesleyan University—Terms Proposed by Socratic Board of Directors, June 1970.

4. *AR*, 1971, Annals 1969–70, xv .

5. E-mail from Don Bruster, June 30, 2006.

6. Telephone interview with Marian Fichtner Morash on April 8, 2006, and supported by Social Security Administration records available on the Internet.

7. SLS letter of March 12, 1971.

8. Undated copy of a presentation certificate on Wesleyan (Department of School Services and Publication) stationery.

9. For help with ideas this section, I am indebted to many fellow Eclectics, but most particularly to Seth F. Kaufman (1970), who experienced both the old and the new Eclectic and shared his perceptions with me in a marathon phone call on May 19, 2006.

10. Constitution of the Eclectic Fraternity, Article 1, Section 2, and Bylaws, Article 11.

11. Letter from A. E. Sunderland Jr. to John Paton, October 2, 1961.

NOTES TO APPENDIX E

1. A letter in the Socratic Literary Society Archives, June 9, 1938, mentioned that Ms. Clark was living in a destitute state and requested monies to help finance a cataract operation for her. A handwritten note on the letter states that she was matron from 1902 through the early 1920s and that she died in Los Angeles in 1950. Socratic Literary Society

Minutes of June 16, 1939, mention that a relief fund for Miss Clark had been set up.

2. Mrs. Thorpe left at midyear. Howard B. Matthews (1928), the undergraduate steward, also served as "matron" for the rest of the year, according to his "Notes for the Eclectic History" in the Paul North Rice Papers.

Belz, Aaron. "Plotting the World's Salvation." *Christianity Today International* 23.1 (Winter 2004): 40, as quoted at http://jmm .aaa.net.au/articles/12769.htm.

Bensinger, Noel E. "Eclectic Frolics and Customs." Memorandum to Eric M. North (undated, but from the 1930s).

Clements, H. Loren, et al. *Songs of Phi Nu Theta—The Eclectic Society.* Middletown, CT: Wesleyan University, 1931.

Dickinson College Web site, http://chronicles.dickinson.edu, accessed 2005.

Eclectic Society. Records, September 7, 1880–June 6, 1970. Eclectic Collection, Olin Library, Wesleyan University, Middletown, CT.

———. Repository, vols. 3 (1867) through 98 (1964). Eclectic Collection, Olin Library, Wesleyan University, Middletown, CT.

———. "The Eclectic Society of Phi Nu Theta—Bylaws, Rules for Regulation of the Library, Order of Initiation, Constitution and Names of the Eclectic Society." Middletown, CT, 1865–1916 and subsequent amendments through 1961, Eclectic Collection, Olin Library, Wesleyan University, Middletown, CT.

Geiges, Edwin J., ed. *Alumni Record of Wesleyan University, 1831–1970.* Middletown, CT, 1971.

Harrower, H. D., S. H. Olin, and W. N. Rice. *Catalogue of the Eclectic Fraternity.* Middletown, CT: Wesleyan University, 1865. Available in Eclectic Collection, Olin Library, Wesleyan University, Middletown, CT.

Muller, Janet Sloan, ed. *Alumni Record of Wesleyan University, 1831– 1980.* Middletown, CT, 1981.

National Governors Association Web site, www.nga.org, accessed 2005.

Ohio Wesleyan University. "Constitution and Rules of Government of the Eclectic *ΦΝΘ* Association Ohio Wesleyan University" (unpublished ms., 1844). Eclectic Collection, Olin Library, Wesleyan University, Middletown, CT.

Patricelli, Leonard J., ed. *The Wesleyan Song Book.* Middletown, CT: Wesleyan University Alumni Council, 1953.

Potts, David B. *Wesleyan University, 1831–1910*. New Haven, CT: Yale University Press, 1992.

Price, Carl F. *Wesleyan's First Century*. Middletown, CT: Wesleyan University, 1932.

Rice, Paul North, E. R. North, and M. B. Crawford. "History of Eclectic" (unpublished ms., 1837–79). Eclectic Collection, Olin Library, Wesleyan University, Middletown, CT.

Scroll, The. Vol. 1 (1926) through unnumbered volume (1976). Eclectic Collection, Olin Library, Wesleyan University, Middletown, CT.

Socratic Literary Society. Records, 1871–1970. Eclectic Collection, Olin Library, Wesleyan University, Middletown, CT.

Stewart, Frederic, and E. M. North. *Phi Nu Theta–Catalogue of the Eclectic Society, 1837–1907*. Middletown, CT: Wesleyan University, 1908.

Wesleyan University Alumni/ae Directory 2000. White Plains, NY: Bernard C. Harris Publishing Company, 2001.

Wesleyan University Alumni Record (AR), 1831–1952. Middletown, CT, 1953.

Wesleyan University Alumni Record (AR), 1831–1961. Middletown, CT, 1962.

Wesleyan University Bulletin, May 1919.

Wesleyan University Web site, www.wesleyan.edu, accessed 2006.

effect of Civil War on, 28ff

first clubhouse, 42

fraternity house at 200 High Street, 55ff

effect of World War I on, 67–68

and Prohibition, 74–75

and the Great Depression, 84–85

effect of World War II on, 92ff

pledging of minority members, 110–11

proposals to abolish, 130–31, 141–42

end of old, 139, 141

purpose of, 145

Eclectic Spring Sing, 100, 103, 132

Eldridge, Donald A., 116

endowment fund, 36–37, 70, 71, 142

English titles (terms), 133, 134

Epistoleus's reports, 95, 98, 117, 125, 131–32, 135, 136–37

Etherington, Edwin D., 10, 111, 136, 193n47

"Evaluation of the Eclectic Fraternity" (essay), 113–14

exclusiveness, 145

executive committee, 56, 112, 124, 137

Exley, Charles E., Jr., 110

extracurricular activities, 39. *See also* athletics; campus/college life, Eclectic participation in

faculty, relations with

Alpha Chapter, 41, 64, 134–35

Beta Chapter, 33

Gamma Chapter, 34–35

faculty guests, 105–6, 112, 119, 134–35

faculty papers in literary exercises, 134–35, 136

Fairchild, Benjamin T., III, 138

Fairchild, Michael M., 138

Farnsworth, Miss, 77

Fauver, Edgar, 79

Fellows, Nathaniel, 33

Ferre (alternately, Ferrie), 16, 17

Fichtner, Eric "The Chief" and Kaethe, 86, 89, 93, 97, 98, 100, 103–5, 107, 120–21, 126–27, 128, 129, 143, 189n27

Fichtner, Marian (Marian Fichtner Morash), 105, 121, 143, 189n27

financial problems/situation (Fraternity), 129, 132, 136

financial problems/situation (Socratic Literary Society), 70–71, 125, 141

fines, 133, 136

finger snapping, 60, 88, 185n17

Fisk, Willbur, 2–3

Forden, David W., 100, 101

foreign students, 89, 92, 101, 118

Fosgate, William A., 28

Foss, Archibald C., 14–15

Foss, Cyrus D., 1, 10, 15, 23, 25, 44, 57

Foss, Cyrus D., Jr., 40

Foss, William J., 15
"Foss Decade," 15
Fox, Philip C., 100
Founders' Prize, 79–80, 90, 91,
    132, 134, 135, app. B
fraternities, growth of at Wes-
    leyan, 17
fraternities, other, relations with,
    78, 109
fraternities, role and functions
    of, 130, 135, 145–46
fraternity dues, 90. *See also* term
    taxes
fraternity house (High Street).
    See also clubhouse (College
    Place)
    planning, construction, and
        dedication, 56ff
    leaks in the roof, 66, 71, 108,
        118
    vines on the walls, 66
    payment of mortgage on, 70
    maintenance, high cost of,
        70–71
    lightning strike, 71
    refurbishment for the cen-
        tennial, 87
    possibility of closing in
        World War II, 94
    discussion about trans-
        forming into dorm/coffee
        house or turning over to
        University, 138, 145–46
    sale of, 141ff
fraternity offices (officers), ixff,
    10, 20–21, 31, 60, 75, 96, 114,
    128, 129, 133, 134, 136, 138

fraternity size, 71, 73, 96, 137. *See
    also* delegations, size of
fraternity songs, 107, app. A. *See
    also* singing tradition
Frost, Richard T., 101
Funk, Peter C., 125

Gamble, David L., 100
gambling, 65
Gamma Chapter, 16, 21, 34–35
Gayer, Alan J., 61
Genesee College, efforts to estab-
    lish a chapter at, 31, 35
Gettier, John A., 194nE-1
Goat Room, 65, 92, 106, 110, 119
Goodale, John H., 7
Goode, Burwell F. (Beta Chapter),
    33
Goode, G. Brown, 39
Gordon, William C., 194n2
Gould, Richard, 98
grace before meals, 104, 105
Greeks, 12
Greek titles (terms), 31, 134, 138,
    145
Gribney Cup, 106
Griscom, N. Thorne, 100
guttering, 76, 77, 99, 101, 105,
    119, 125
Gwillim, Rhys B., 37

Harriman, Daniel G., 29, 45
Harriman, Henry I., 45, 87
Harrington, Calvin S., 38
Harris, Philip B., 97
Harrison, Ralph C., 15–16, 23
Harrower, Henry D., 6, 30, 31, 39

ABOUT THE AUTHOR

William B. B. Moody, a member of the Eclectic Society of Phi Nu Theta, graduated from Wesleyan University in 1959. He currently lives in Maryland, where he is the head of the foreign language department at Sandy Springs Friends School.